AMAZON FBA 2020

A COMPLETE GUIDE ON HOW TO START A SUCCESSFUL ONLINE BUSINESS AND MAKE PASSIVE INCOME SELLING ON AMAZON: MAKE MONEY ONLINE AND WORK FROM HOME

By: Roger H. Neeley

Table of Contents

INTRODUCTION

For the longest time, eBay was the only place where items could be sold online. While eBay is great, it requires a lot of work from your side: procurement, SEO, shipping, customer care and so on. These days, more digital marketplaces have sprung up and one of them is the Amazon sales program called FBA. FBA means Fulfillment By Amazon and it is a distribution company (A distribution company offers storage and shipping services for its customers' products).

Fulfillment By Amazon is unique because Amazon is also the market for these items and therefore has an active interest in the items being sold. What makes FBA even more extraordinary is that its items are also eligible for Amazon mail-order advertising, including Free Super Saver Shipping and Amazon Prime. To get into it however, it is important to understand how FBA works and how other companies use FBA.

Amazon buyers use Prime to receive free shipping. You spend slightly more on things like spices, coffee, tea, socks, toilet paper, towels, detergents and so on. They spend a lot more because they trust Amazon completely. It's good for sellers because it means you earn more and sell more.

Amazon controls Internet trading very well and raises the bar for its customers, suppliers and owners. Customer service is essential to them and we use it with Fulfillment by Amazon. As a product vendor, you do not have to worry about customer service after the sale. You just have to send more products to Amazon and they do the rest.

How do you configure an account for FBA?

1. Open an Amazon account

If you've never bought or sold on Amazon, and you do not have an account yet, just go to the Amazon website and click on the sell Amazon link at the bottom of the page- it will take you to another page from which you can sign up.

2. Set up your Amazon account

If you have an Amazon sales account, contact Amazon Customer Support to set up your account for FBA. If you have an FBA representative in your account, you can solve any future problems. The representative will guide you through your first delivery.

At this point, you have done your due diligence and you have an FBA account.

One of the questions many ask is "What is Amazon FBA?". To help explain what Amazon FBA is, let's take a quick look at how Amazon FBA can help you take your online sales business to the next level.

Amazon FBA or Fulfillment By Amazon is an Amazon-based program that lets you save and then send your items to Amazon (and sell them on the Amazon website). Amazon FBA is very simple but powerful at the same time and can lift your business to a higher level at a very low cost.

Imagine a scene where you have searched for products and picked up books, DVDs, household items, and beautiful new toys (yes, items sold through Amazon FBA must be new or collectable). But you have to stop stocking products because there's no room left in your house. This is where the Amazon FBA comes into play.

All that is required is for you to scan or list the items as usual in your Amazon sales account. With only a few clicks, you can print barcodes that you must insert using the Amazon's original barcode item (for items with barcode) or listed on the Amazon website). Just a few more clicks and you print a delivery note that needs to be sent to the box (s). You then book support from a freight forwarder. Then finish the order and wait for the order to be picked up. A few days later, your item will be in Amazon for sale and you can sit back and transfer your money. Amazon FBA processes payments, shipments and emails from customers.

Yes, Amazon charges extra, but these are low and you get fantastic savings on postage. You use Amazon's purchasing power and there are no queues left at post offices and you do not have to buy bubble wrap and more boxes.

Another thing you should understand is that you can use Amazon FBA to ship your order to eBay and other buyers. And at very low cost and in most cases much cheaper than you can. All pricing information is available on your country's Amazon web site. Just search for Amazon FBA.

Truly, you have nothing to lose and a lot to win by signing up for the Amazon FBA account.

Amazon's FBA program is an amazing opportunity for the general public but especially for entrepreneurs (particularly those who start as a one-man shop). The special thing about Amazon FBA is its scalability. As a one-man shop, you can compete with the biggest and most established sellers. Small businesses are limited in space and time management to sell, list, place, and ship orders. You can run both small jobs (eg 20 per day) and larger jobs (eg 100,000 per day). This is reflected in the fact that you can start with Amazons

Fulfillment as a small shop and flourish as a larger company. You can now efficiently manage the increased volume as you manage your inventory and source your product.

This reduces the competitive advantage with the largest seller and allows you to generate real income and grow as big as you want. Think about it. You only have to access the products of your choice. Amazon FBA provides a source of revenue that can take you to a whole new level. In any distribution center (Amazon has more than 65) you commit to low contract costs, a staff that supports the processing of the order, its shipping and the customer.

All you have to do is get your products, spend your time editing and packaging them, and send them to Amazon.

Some of the main advantages of Amazon FBA include:

1. You have access to millions of Prime customers
2. Change order management and integrate and extend logistics on Amazon
3. Sell worldwide with the FBA export program to access your customers around the world at no additional cost.
4. The Multi-Channel Fulfillment Option (MCF) is an optional FBA program that lets you easily run world-class Amazon distribution centers for orders outside of Amazon... and take a paid vacation while

FBA works for you to respond to customer orders and manage customer service.

These facts below will also help you understand how FBA can help improve your market share:

- FBA now accounts for 45% of Amazon's revenue growth
- Amazon Prime was launched in 2005 and in 2009, Prime had 2 million members. in 2011 it was more than 5 million; in 2014 there are more than 20 million members
- Premium currently represents only 6% of the total number of Amazon customers.
- The premium increases by more than 20% compared to the previous year
- Regular customers spend 140% more than regular Amazon customers
- 40% to 50% of Amazon customers have never bought from third parties

With FBA, Amazon can help you increase your online sales and satisfy your customers. At the same time, you can save valuable time and focus on growing your business.

With Amazon FBA, you can ensure that your products are sold and shipped directly to customers, so you will not have to bother and worry about shipping and processing. This can also be of great benefit to companies that do not have enough storage space for their products as they host their products locally.

However, Fulfillment By Amazon is essentially the ideal component for all sellers. Before you sign up, make sure you're bidding the right way by determining how your products reach your customers, how you control the process, and how scalable the program is.

HOW YOUR PRODUCTS REACH AMAZON PRIME CUSTOMERS

The most important component of selling with Fulfillment By Amazon is how your products reach Amazon Prime customers. If you use Amazon FBA, all your customers can choose a free two-day shipping with an Amazon Prime account. In addition to premium customers, Amazon regular customers will receive free shipping on orders over 35.00 USD. One of the key benefits of the FBA list is that your products are listed on Amazon Prime customers at no shipping cost, so you can increase your sales.

What is Amazon FBA Seller Central?

Amazon FBA Seller Central is the aspect of the Amazon website that allows you to fully control the warehouse where your items are stored, the listing of your items, and the display of the selling characteristics of your items. Products. It is essentially a complete dashboard dedicated to your products and their public perception. You can search for adding your products, view other prices from competing FBA sellers, and determine what steps Amazon should take at the time of sale, such as: B. when shipping products. The centralized vendor is critical to the sales process as it provides the "first impression" your customers receive when they find your products.

What is the scalability of Amazon FBA?

The scalability of Amazon FBA is another important factor to consider when working with Amazon. As your business grows, you want to make sure Amazon grows with you to make each order run efficiently. With the scalability of the program, you can be sure that Amazon can help you in the high season and offer more resources as you sell more products. With the ability to pack and ship a single unit or thousands of different units, the possibilities are endless.

For starters, the Amazon FBA program means fulfillment by Amazon. This is an Amazon-provided service that enables online and offline vendors to send their products to Amazon. Amazon packs and ships the products on your behalf to individual customers. You may not know how big the Amazon market is if you do not visit it regularly. They have grown so much, from selling books to selling almost everything.

You can also sell products through Amazon and not use their FBA service. So you can ship your own products. However, using the FBA system has many benefits that will save you time and provide a more automated business solution.

This is actually a service similar to other direct mailers, but Amazon keeps your own goods in one of its distribution centers. The service will ship your goods anytime, anywhere on your behalf. This system can be further integrated into your website to create a virtually fully automatic system for shipping your goods to Amazon and shipping via Amazon. The service costs are very competitive and you pay only for storage and actual shipments. At reduced Amazon rates, they charge no fee for using the system.

Why should you consider the Amazon system?

Here are some key points of the FBA system:

- You can sell almost anything on Amazon or on your own website and have them packed and shipped.
- By automating your website with Amazon, your business can run with the autopilot, and you can take

your time if you want, and your business always works.

- Send all your shares on Amazon and they will manage everything, you just have to collect your profits.
- Amazon outperforms eBay in terms of traffic and is a major competitor to eBay.
- Some eBay sellers use the Amazon FBA to ship products sold through eBay.

What can you sell?

You can sell virtually anything, as I said before. For example, in addition to books, Amazon has categories similar to eBay that cover almost everything you can imagine for home, garden, office, clothing, sports, and more.

With the FBA program and significant traffic generated by Amazon, you can build an Amazon WebStore, find products for sale, and quickly get started with an online business using the tools provided. This way has been proven to be one of the easiest ways to open an online business.

Amazon.com is the largest online marketplace and the platform continues to grow. It offers online retailers tremendous opportunities to sell their products to countless consumers. When you sell on Amazon.com, you're probably choosing the best way. However, if you only bid on Amazon, you run the risk of losing more product sales. It may seem difficult to expand to other systems, but since you already sell on Amazon.com, you can easily use other platforms to increase your revenue, such as the Amazon FBA platform.

Amazon.com offers a multi-channel processing option (MCF) that allows you to expand your business to more distribution platforms at no additional cost.

What is Amazon Multi-Channel Fulfillment?

Amazon's FBA support meets your Amazon orders and chooses MCF to make purchases from all other systems. You can delegate the most power to Amazon. Regardless of where you sell items - on auction sites, on Shopify, or on another platform, Amazon selects the products and passes them on to your customers. You are only required to pay the shipping costs.

Multi-ChannelFulfillment allows you to choose a regular delivery within two days or the next day. It also calculates shipping and shipping costs based on the size of the item and the selected shipping method.

If you want to use Amazon.com's Multi-Channel Fulfilment, you must consider some requirements. First, you must be licensed for FBA. This means that you have registered credit cards with Amazon. These cards will certainly be charged for execution costs unless your seller account has a positive balance after the stability fees have been removed from FCM fees.

You should also have a professional seller account on Amazon to use MCF, which usually costs $ 39. However, you do not pay the fees for the product list every month.

Use Amazon's MCF with these guidelines:

The Amazon MCF is an excellent strategy for online stores as long as you can use FBA and meet the above requirements. But there are however some tools that can ease the situation even better for you and your customers.

Use messaging on goods receipt forms

For Amazon MCF, the logos and customizations are limited. You can not understand custom inserts or wrappers. It is possible that special messages are printed on the packaging film. Use these special messages to show that you value your customers' business and value them as customers.

Change prices depending on the platform

One good thing about selling through multiple channels is that you can plan prices to increase your sales. For example, if you offer a product on Amazon, it can be cost-effective to be competitive. The same product on another system that is not as competitive and therefore can cost more.

Book some benefits

This trick has a commercial meaning wherever you sell products online. You can never tell when unpredictable costs can arise. However, with MCF pricing can be profitable. You may have to pay for shipping and administration, consumables, and account charges. Even if you pass these costs to customers, it is usually wise to spend money on a quality item that needs to be quickly listed in other product channels.

Selling on multiple systems ensures that your products are perceived by a wider audience. The Amazon FBA platform makes it quick and easy. Now that you know how it works and know some of the best tips, you can download the full Amazon FBA Guide and start selling.

The principles of Low / High Buy are very effective online! You can easily join the online money-rush by applying the very simple principles of low-level buying/selling at a high level!

Fulfillment By Amazon generates real profits from locally purchased ordinary items.

RETAIL ARBITRAGE AND AMAZON FBA

Retail arbitrage is not a novel idea, but has gained new meaning as a market with the Internet. You can easily buy locally-priced items at discount stores/pharmacies and resell them to Amazon FBA.

The concept is a simple one. A retail store (Walmart, Target, etc) puts up a product for sale at a certain price. You buy it and resell it at a higher price.

Retail arbitrage is a great way to earn money without taking extraordinary steps. Imagine, if you only use a regional sale, it means that you are getting a market that people around the country or around the world can not access. Your savings can become your Cash Cow!

Categories of items for sale with retail arbitrage

The possibilities are really limitless if you think about it. You can sell everything from food to lingerie. To succeed, all you need to do is to know the market for retail items and enter that market. The categories of items sold with retail arbitrage are almost everything you would buy in a typical brick building.

You can even sell used items on Amazon! Some items are not approved for sale on Amazon. Things like dangerous objects and other objects that are subject to restrictions. For more information, visit the Amazon website.

Using Amazon FBA

Once you use Amazon FBA to sell your items, you'll easily understand why it works with FBA shipping. The process is easy to start. You pay a small fee as a seller. Decide which items you want to use on Amazon and send it to Amazon.

You do not have to find the buyers, because Amazon is known worldwide and has more than 100 million visitors daily. Plus, you do not have to bother and worry about shipping every single sale, but Amazon does it for you. You only need to register, pay the fees and ship your items.

A small initial investment of a few hundred dollars to buy your stock AND joining the FBA can be very profitable.

Did you realize that Amazon is not the seller of anything on Amazon? Did you know that everyday people like you and me can sell physical products on Amazon? This option is not novel - it has been around for some time, but it is becoming increasingly popular due to the increasing frequency of training.

There are three ways to sell physical products on Amazon:

1. Sell the products of others on Amazon and ship the orders yourself;
2. Sell other people's products on Amazon
3. let Amazon send and sell your own products and let them ship from Amazon.

The first means called merchant filled. You publish your goods on the Amazon website, but you place orders or send them yourself. The last two ways are called FBA.

The satisfied retailer is the simplest and cheapest entry but requires much more work. You list your products on the Amazon site. When purchasing the products, you are responsible for shipping the products to the buyer. With this method, you can even sell things that you have in the house.

You may also use FBA to sell other people's products. In this case, go to the store and search for products that are already sold on Amazon. You buy them, you write your own UPC label on the product, you create it, you make the list and send it to an Amazon department store and you are waiting for the buyer.

There are smartphone apps that you can use to analyze products before you buy them to see if you can make a profit. If you enjoy shopping, doing good business, and shipping a box, this may be your business. The other advantage of using FBA is that your products are eligible for the Amazon Prime program. Those who attend can benefit from a free shipping within 2 days. Many people are open to paying a little more for a product.

Another way to use the FBA program is to sell your own products. You can find a product you can sell, find a private label maker, create your own brand and sell your product. This is the most lucrative way to sell on Amazon. However, this initially requires more capital. It's also riskier because you have to order the inventory.

As you can now see, selling on Amazon is definitely one thing you can do to earn extra income or become a full-time business. If you desire to open an online store or add an extra source of revenue to your existing online business, you should definitely consider the FBA.

HOW AMAZON FBA WORKS

Amazon FBA (Fulfillment By Amazon) is a business opportunity offered by Amazon to encourage business owners to list their products in their market.

The model works from Amazon and gives users the ability to send their products to their warehouse and have them "filled" by a giant's reserve after a successful purchase (he sends them).

Part of the reason why Amazon does this is to buy niche products that are both unique and valuable (they own the products - they only ship them to you), and partly to use their huge infrastructure (for what they do) would pay any case). This also contributes to their offer as a company, as they can add an even wider range of products to their portfolio (which is practically their main competitive advantage).

For the FBA model, it is important to consider that it reflects the new "digital" corporate culture, which seems to have increased even more after the 2008 crash. Businesses have turned to the Internet and social media to find buyers and start lean companies.

Gone are the days when traders determined the fate of the products. Now, new businesses, entrepreneurs, and ordinary citizens can earn more than $ 10,000 in income per month without having to own land. All infrastructures, marketing and realization are managed by a fully independent company (Amazon) - where you only have to procure a high-performance product.

To determine if you want to use this investment method, I've created this tutorial to explain the process of using Amazon FBA. Rather than trying to cope with the remnants of a local market, the new "digital" empire with all its promises is one of the best ways to break into the new business world.

How does this work?

All companies work in the same way: they buy/build a product, offer it to a market, and any "profit" that you can make can be used either for life or for reinvestment in more / better products.

Most people have two problems: 1) They have no product. 2) You have no access to a market.

Although both problems are legitimate - which would have been a major drawback without the "digital" medium - the times have gone so far that entry barriers are so low that it is enough to invest multiple times. $ 1,000 for sale to a global audience.

And despite the fact that the "Amazon" option has existed for almost 10 years (anyone can list products on its market), the "FBA" model (which is truly autonomous) has begun to become popular in the last 24 years, past years. Months or more.

If you have not gone to Business School to explain briefly how to run a "successful" business, you need to be able to provide a product/service to a broad audience. As a rule, you aim for a net profit margin of about 30% (after expenses and advertising costs). The way you do this depends on you: the key is to buy low, to sell high.

Well, not because the "digital" field is big, do the "markets" work normally. Competition is obviously a great force, as well as the idea that, because it is "simple", something can be replicated in a relatively simple way by others (resulting in an erosion of your profits).

Selling to Amazon typically works by providing access to products that users can not access locally or that have local access but that present significant limitations (such as color/size issues) or reliability issues. In other words, while the Amazon market is huge, you do not believe that you can thwart supply and demand.

The real trick with "digital" companies is to provide access to unique products (usually made by you or your company) that are only available through you. These products should aim to provide a solution that most people have no idea about, and therefore legitimize the proposal to buy them over the Internet.

Obviously, creating a "unique" product is 1000 times easier to say than to do. The trick is to find solutions to your own problems. Work on refining a range of skills that you can provide to a wider audience, and identify "products" that can be created and offered to simplify/resolve the issues that have arisen.

To sell on Amazon, you need to do the following:

Register the Amazon Seller Account

The first step is to open a "Seller Account" on Amazon. There are two types of seller accounts: "Individual" and "Professional". Individual is free and will permit you to list articles already in the Amazon catalog. Every time you sell a product, you pay a small fee. The cost of the business is $ 40 per month and does not include "per-sale" costs (although other fees such as storage fees, etc. may apply). This is the only account that lets you list new Amazon catalog items.

Register for GS1

Allows you to create * barcodes *. They exist in two formats: UPC (Universal Product Code) and EAN (European Article Number). Although these are cheap to buy (US $ 10), Amazon, Google and eBay strongly recommend using GS1 for standardization. By using GS1, your products will be recognized by Amazon. The downside is the cost, but that should not really matter. We always recommend spending about $ 500 on administration fees, which would definitely be one.

Creating a Legal Business (Optional)

If you want to set up a real FBA transaction, you need a legal business (and a bank account). Not only does this give Amazon the opportunity to open a business account, it also gives you better tax management (which is notoriously bad for investing your own money on a personal basis). The installation is very simple but only required if you really only want to work with Amazon on an FBA basis. If you want to sell products on the system, you can do so under your own name.

Buy / Build Packaging

You then need to purchase a range of product packaging. If you make the product yourself, you must package it in standardized cardboard boxes. Since there are many possibilities, we will simply say that you should look for a boxing/printing company that will do it for you. There are many who are capable of it. You must also follow Amazon's instructions for acceptable types of packaging.

Sending Products to Amazon

Once you have the products in the box, you must send them to Amazon. This is organized through the Amazon sales system, so you can choose a time when products need to go to the Amazon warehouse. Again, due to variations in the process, it is best to follow Amazon's instructions.

Start selling

This is the hardest part explained below. The last step is to sell the products. This is the hardest because you are almost exclusively exposed to the market (Amazon and any other market you could bring to the platform).

The trick to buying products from Amazon is effective marketing. Marketing goes to several points. The most notable thing is that you need to be able to grab the attention of potential buyers and then create a demand that gives them the opportunity to buy your product to meet that demand.

Although there are numerous ways to do this, you need to remember that if you want to do it efficiently, you need to be able to market it regardless of whether it's popular with Amazon or not. The less Amazon you need, the more likely you are to convince people to buy through this channel.

In later chapters, you will learn more about marketing your products.

NOTE

Finally, we must stress that sales made by you should NOT be considered an absolute benefit. Your profit comes only when your other costs have been taken into account (like the products themselves, the cards and the marketing). It's a novice mistake to think that the money you receive from Amazon is actually your "home" profit - this is not the case.

You have to build your initial principle from the gross income and then decide what you want to do with the profits you've made (as already mentioned - in the form of a deductible or the reintroduction of better / more numerous products).

To be financially successful, you have to work very hard and there is no solution. You must plan at least 40 to 50 hours per week to earn an active income. But what if I tell you that you can make a living while you sleep? Too good to be true, right? But it is true, even if it takes a bit of time, but anything that is worth it takes time. In your spare time you can earn passive income.

The basic concept of Fulfillment by Amazon is like all Amazon concepts easy ... although there are many back-and-forth concepts that I will review later. With this service, you send the products you want to sell directly to Amazon (your inventory, as Amazon calls it). Whether books, CDs, clothes, computer accessories, toys or anything else. They store it for you in their camp. As soon as orders have been received, Amazon selects the product, packs it and sends it directly to your customers.

You can use Fulfillment by Amazon if you have only a few products for sale on Amazon or if you want to sell thousands of products. You can use it if you start a new business or if you want to have an existing business that you want to switch to Fulfillment by Amazon.

You can use Fulfillment to send any items you sell to Amazon or items you sell elsewhere to Amazon. This is what Amazon calls Multi-Channel Fulfillment. One more thing: if you use Fulfillment by Amazon, you do not have to fill everything with Amazon. You may use it for some products and not for others.

Let us take a look at the advantages and disadvantages of Fulfillment by Amazon:

- You benefit from the reputation of Amazon. Amazon is a brand recognized by customers around the world. When they order a product sent by Amazon, they know they are getting it. And fast. And they know that they can give it back if they

37

wish. It can make a big difference if they decide to buy from you.

- You can offer a faster service. Amazon has a state-of-the-art online order fulfillment and fulfillment service. They may bring your products to your buyers faster than you.

- Your products may be better rated on Amazon. For a Fulfillment by Amazon item, your item is most often displayed at the top of the search. Unclaimed products from Amazon sellers are listed by the total cost (product price plus postage), but your items are listed by price only. You can often rate your items at a price that approximates the lowest overall price, possibly the first item on the list and attracting more buyers.

- Your customers receive free shipping. If you use Amazon Fulfillment, your customers will benefit from the free delivery of their products with Super Saver Delivery or Amazon Prime. This can give you a big edge over sellers who do not use Fulfillment by Amazon.

- Reduce Overhead You have to do the numbers, but in most cases there can be good cost savings. FBA eliminates the need for space or staff to complete picking/shipping and associated administration. It could even mean lowering your prices, selling more real estate, and earning more money at the same time.

- You can be much more productive. I think that's the biggest potential benefit. When you use FBA, you do not have to waste time sorting, storing, picking up and packing goods. Amazon does it for you. You can also manage customer service, returns, and so on. That means you can spend most of your time marketing and selling things that make you money. And because you can spend more time with it, at least theoretically you should be able to make more money.

Well, although Amazon tells you that there is no problem with FBA, I think there is a list of things you must keep in mind:

- It is not so good for products that take a long time to sell or that have not yet been proven because you have to pay a monthly storage fee as long as your products are available on Amazon.
- The use of FBA can make it difficult to compete with other sellers, especially those who also use FBA. How do you want to differentiate your product and service from those?
- This is the main disadvantage of Fulfillment by Amazon, in my opinion. Your business depends almost entirely on Amazon. What happens if something goes wrong? For example, if your

systems fail and do not respond to your orders or if you lose your inventory? Or if they raise their prices? And if, after placing your product in an Amazon box, the buyer decides to return to Amazon next time?

- When you sign up for Fulfillment by Amazon at Amazon.com, you can only sell products in the UK. Which seems a bit odd, if you consider that the Internet should be a global business method. In some Amazon countries (Germany, France, USA and Japan) you can sell with Fulfillment by Amazon. However, you have to register separately. At first, you probably would not want that, but it could be a way to expand in the future.

Let us now see how you use Fulfillment by Amazon.

At this point, I should say that there is a wealth of detailed information on how the Amazon website works. But it is very difficult and many difficult things to follow. I will try to give you a simple and user-friendly summary of Fulfillment by Amazon.

First, Amazon compliance is no different than other methods of using Amazon. It is fully integrated into it. You have just set up for sale on the Amazon Marketplace as usual and then select the desired products at FBA.

Getting started with Amazon Marketplace is very easy. You may not need to register in advance - you can open a seller account when you list your first product. To register as a seller, you need a company name, an address, a display name (which may be your company name or something else), a credit card, and a telephone number. It's everything you need to get started.

Amazon offers two methods of sale: sell a little or sell a lot.

Basically, "a little bit" is for occasional and hobby sellers who want to sell less than 35 items per month. It costs 86 pence plus a referral fee for each sale and you can not sell in all categories of Amazon. Selling "a lot" is for companies that expect to sell more than 35 items a month. You pay a monthly flat fee of £ 28.75 and removal fees. You can sell in all categories of Amazon products. The option "Sell a little" is not really useful at Fulfillment by Amazon.

To take full advantage of Fulfillment by Amazon, you also need to become what Amazon calls a Pro Merchant provider. Professional traders have access to volume and wholesale tools. A web interface makes managing your product descriptions, inventories and orders easier. You can also export and import information to and from your account. Typically, the Pro Merchant option costs you a lot less money, allowing you to work on smaller margins and make money from products and sales. Who sells "a bit", can not.

Easy access, unlimited choice and fast processing are some of the infinite charms of e-commerce. Intelligently exploited, these factors can be of benefit to both buyers and sellers. To attract buyers and generate significant revenue, online retailers must meet the widely anticipated needs of e-commerce. Respond to all market demands and focus on every detail of your business. This can be hectic for any online retailer. In this case, you need additional help with organizing your day-to-day business and ensuring that everything runs smoothly. Fulfillment by Amazon is one of those sophisticated web services that provide valuable assistance to merchants by professionally executing the complex and responsive fulfillment process on their behalf.

Fulfillment by Amazon (FBA) is a highly functional program that provides vendors with storage for their inventory and orders through the Amazon Distribution Center. In all areas of e-commerce, immediate storage and regular execution are critical to business development, customer satisfaction and profit maximization. FBA offers individuals, small businesses and large enterprises the ability to exceed their customers' expectations through secure, intelligent and fast delivery of orders. Now, as a manufacturer or wholesaler, you can keep a close eye on your purchases and production as FBA eliminates the need for your own warehouse and high placement costs. You do not even have to worry about packing and shipping the product, regardless of the size or frequency of orders.

The Amazon execution system may seem complicated, but in practice it is very easy to understand as it is comprehensively designed to meet current commercial demands and the latest trends in e-commerce. Once you have sent your new or used products to the distribution center, they will be stored in Amazon warehouses and can be shipped immediately. Amazon initiates order processing for your products upon receipt of customer orders via its own website or on your direct request for shipping. After this procedure, the specified items are removed from the inventory and packaged for shipping. Finally, ordered goods are shipped from Amazon distribution centers to these destinations. After the deduction of the execution fee, the net amount of the sale will be credited to your account and the same process repeated for subsequent transactions. You can be sure that all necessary steps are automatically performed transparently and professionally by the most reliable, efficient and experienced hands of Amazon.

It should be noted, however, that the FBA holdings are owned and controlled by the seller. Because there is no upper or lower inventory limit, you can always add or remove your products from the supply stores. Similarly, the frequency of orders is irrelevant, since the execution costs are deducted only at the point of sale. Other FBA features include order fulfillment, insurance and automatic tracking. In the end, what can be concluded is that Fulfillment by Amazon requires you to focus on your production, sales, and management without having to worry about executing your orders.

Buyers will know that your item is in stock. When a buyer sees an FBA list, he knows that the product is in stock and shipped directly from the Amazon warehouse. Other sellers than FBA can cancel an order for a variety of reasons. However, with FBA, the buyer can be sure that this is not the case. This is especially important during the holiday season when buyers expect to receive their orders as soon as possible. There is nothing worse than an annoyed buyer because he did not receive his item in time for the holidays. By using the Amazon order, shoppers know that the item is packaged professionally and arrives on time.

FBA articles are eligible for Amazon Prime.

Prime is a service that allows free unlimited shipping within 2 days for all Amazon purchases and costs $ 79 per year. In addition to Amazon's own articles, third-party FBA articles are also eligible for Prime. This means that your company has access to some of Amazon's best customers. Preferred customers buy many items, especially during the holiday season. Premium customers love free shipping! When you use FBA, you have an advantage over other sellers who do not use it because a buyer who receives the Prime service often chooses your item at the expense of a contest that is not FBA-driven. You can receive your item with a two-day free shipping that you can not get without FBA competition.

You spend less time with customer service.

FBA manages the entire customer service for your buyers. To put it simply, if your buyer has a problem with their order, they can contact Amazon directly for assistance. You can save yourself so much time and hassle if you do not have to manage your own customer service.

If you're a third-party Amazon reseller, using FBA will give you more time to focus on the most important aspect of your business: finding a new inventory. With more time to find a good inventory, your company's profits should increase significantly!

To reiterate, here are the steps to open the Amazon Seller Account:

1. Open an Amazon Seller account - Choose a seller category, create your Amazon seller account, and set up your seller profile.
2. List your products - List products already available on Amazon or list new products.

3. Manage your inventory - Maintain inventory levels to compete with other sellers and consider sponsoring specific products as needed.
4. Execute and send orders - Decide between shipping by the seller or its execution by Amazon.
5. Receive your earnings - Amazon deducts the cost of your winnings and sends the balance to your bank account.

If you are a small-business owner who is offering a unique product, we'll bet you're considering selling to Amazon. Amazon is a proven powerhouse for retail, and third-party providers account for most of this growth. By the end of 2019, a lot more than 70% of the company's sales are expected to be generated on the Amazon market.

On the one hand, Amazon offers sellers a large audience of potential customers. With Amazon's comprehensive suite of management and sales tools, sellers can also save far more than they can do on their own. In addition to having to sell hardware products to capitalize on Amazon's amazing market, Amazon Home Services allows B2C service providers to network and connect with customers in their respective regions.

If you want to use the Amazon Marketplace to grow your small business, read our full and detailed guide to selling to Amazon. We've also put together tips on best sellers on

Amazon and tips from leading Amazon vendors so that you can maximize your use of the Amazon market.

Although entire books have been written about selling on Amazon, selling your products on the market can be a really quick and easy process.

Successful Amazon vendors include nationally recognized brands, with individual vendors shipping thousands of units directly from their salon and everything in between. It all varies, based on how you use the Amazon market and various services to meet the needs of your small business.

Regardless of size, each new Amazon salesperson starts with the same five steps. To reiterate. here are some of the details you need to know to sell on Amazon.

STEP 1: OPEN AN AMAZON SELLER ACCOUNT

To set up your Amazon seller account and sell it to Amazon, you must select a seller category, provide information about your business, and understand Amazon's sales rules.

STEP 2: CHOOSE A SELLER CATEGORY

When you sign up to sell to Amazon, choose one of the following three sales categories, depending on the size of your business:

Amazon retailers: If you own a very small business and you want to sell fewer than 40 items a month, you can sign up as a retailer on Amazon. It only costs you $ 0.99 per sale plus a few other transaction fees.

Amazon Pro Seller: If you desire to sell more than 40 items per month, you'll need to create a Pro Account. Amazon charges a subscription fee of $ 39.99 per month plus a transaction fee for each sale.

Amazon sellers: If you make products yourself, you can sell these products to Amazon as a wholesaler. They take care of the list of products, their execution and shipping, and when they are out of stock, order more.

Note that some products must be approved for sale and, if approved, only sellers with Pro accounts can sell those products. Some licensed products include specialized software, laser pointers, and hoverboards. Before you select the type of account you want to connect to, read the full list of Amazon products that require special permission to determine if you need the green light to become a seller. In addition, Amazon prohibits the sale of certain items, such as prescription drugs, on its platform. Therefore, check these restrictions as well.

STEP 3: CREATE YOUR AMAZON SELLER ACCOUNT

After selecting the category you want to sell to, you can set up your Amazon Seller account. To finish setting up your account, Amazon asks:

Your Company Name - This is the name visible to customers on the Amazon Marketplace.

Your legal name and address: This information will be stored in your account as a reference for Amazon. If you are a registered company or have a fictitious company name or database administrator, use the specific name and address under which you are registered.

Contact Information: Amazon uses your contact information to send you order notifications, warranty claims, and service and technical updates. Customers use their contact information to answer questions about their orders. The contact details for Amazon and customers can be the same or separate. Where are the products delivered? Although your shipper's location does not change the shipping time or shipping costs for buyers, some customers use this information to make a purchase decision between similar ads.

Bank Account Information: Amazon directly charges payments for products that are sold every 14 days to your bank account.

Shipping Options: Select the regions of the world you want to ship to and specify if you want to speed shipping.

STEP 4: SET UP YOUR SALESPERSON PROFILE

Once your account is set up, the next step in selling to Amazon is to complete your public seller profile. Think of the Amazon salesperson profile as your Amazon-based social networking profile for your business, where Amazon customers can get to know your business, review your shipping and returns policies, read customer reviews, and more.

Here are the main sections that you would have to fill out immediately in your salesperson profile:

About the seller section: Introduce your small business to buyers. Tell them who you are, how you started your business, share your business philosophy, and add more information that can help the buyer establish an emotional connection to you as a salesperson.

Logo of your provider: Customers will see your logo on your preview page, in your store-front and on the "Offer List" page. Your logo should be 120 x 30 pixels and the image may not contain a URL or a reference to your own website.

Return and Refund Policy: Tell the customer how to return items, including the address to which the goods should be returned, and tell the customer when the refund will be processed. However, please note that sellers are required under Amazon's policy to allow the return for at least 30 days.

Once you've provided all this information, you can access your Seller Central dashboard, list products, and sell on Amazon.

STEP 5: LIST YOUR PRODUCTS

There is a learning way to determine how to sell successfully on Amazon. But once you understand it, selling on Amazon can be easy and intuitive. Once you have set up this seller account, you can put your products up for sale on the Amazon Marketplace.

If you are a single seller, list your products one by one on the Amazon Marketplace. However, if you are a commercial seller, you can list your products in bulk. Some types of products, such as clothing, support size or color variations can be listed in a single list.

The products you sell on Amazon fall into one of two categories: products that are already listed on the Amazon Marketplace, and new products where you are the first or only seller.

LISTING PRODUCTS ALREADY ON AMAZON

If the product you list is already on Amazon, you can use the pictures and descriptions available on the website. All that is required is that you stipulate the number of products for sale, describe their condition, and select the available shipping options.

If the inventory is exhausted with other sellers selling the same product, your ad will show up on Amazon. Also, remember to differentiate yourself from other suppliers who have listed the same product. You can offer free shipping, faster delivery or lower prices to differentiate yourself from other sellers.

You'll find "List New Product" in your vendor's dashboard. Browse the product catalog to see if Amazon already saves it. You will be asked to provide prices, quantity, and shipping information. You can add one product each. However, if you list more than 50 products that are already in the Amazon catalog, use Excel to populate and download the UPC / EAN codes for your listed products.

LISTING A PRODUCT NOT YET ON AMAZON

Do you design or build a brand new product that is not yet available on Amazon? The good news is that you will certainly have less competition. The worst news? Publishing new products requires an Amazon Pro account and a few extra steps.

TO LIST A NEW PRODUCT ON AMAZON, YOU MUST PROVIDE THE FOLLOWING:

The UPC / EAN number: This is a unique 12- or 13-digit barcode for product tracking. Multiple lists of different sellers of the same product have a single UPC / EAN number, and only a detailed product list is created that matches this unique number.

SKU: This refers to a special number that you create to track each of your ads.

The product should be described in as short a manner as possible.

Product Description and Benchmarks: Use bullets as a quick descriptive text to grab the attention of the buyer. In the product description, you can give a more comprehensive overview of your product.

Product images: High-quality images are essential for successful sales on Amazon. At Amazon, images must be at least 500 x 500 pixels in size and on a white background with no text or watermarks. The product must occupy at least 80% of the image area. For optimal results, use well-saturated images of at least 1,000 x 1,000 pixels.

Keywords: For each new product listed, Amazon offers five fields of 50 characters each, listing the search terms.

Your product description and pictures are your time to shine! Make sure the description for search engines is optimized and that you include images of high-quality products. Once you've collected the information about your product, there are two ways to download new product lists:

- If you sell 50 or fewer products, you can use the Add Supplier tool.

- To add multiple products that are not yet listed in the Amazon catalog, follow these steps:

1 Go to the seller Central

1 Download the Excel template of the inventory file that corresponds to your main product category.

1 Fill in all the details of your products from a single spreadsheet and download them.

You can also link certain e-commerce applications, such as Shopify and BigCommerce, to your Amazon Seller account to automatically track product lists.

Customer lists may be available immediately after the end of your download. It may take up to 24 hours for Amazon to process your download. If you do not see your new listing right away on the listing page, be patient and come back the following day for regular updates. If it still appears to be missing, contact Amazon through the seller's portal or use the FAQ to fix download errors.

STEP 6: MANAGE YOUR INVENTORY

Once you have your ads downloaded and set up live on the Amazon Marketplace, you can direct all aspects of your seller account on the Seller Central website: search for new orders, update your inventory, and monitor your performance statistics, etc.

Properly taking care of your inventory is one of the most important factors for a successful sale on Amazon. As a buyer, think about how you feel when you click on a product that you want or really need, but find that it is out of stock. This is a great missed opportunity for the seller.

To stop this from happening, you can use different tools. The simplest for small sellers is the manufacturer dashboard. From there, you can manually adjust the inventory of all your products. If you are a professional seller, you can also adjust your stock levels with an Excel mass download. If you use an Amazon-integrated inventory app, such as Vendio or SellerEngine, you can use it to update your Amazon inventory.

Sometimes sellers sponsor their products with ads when a particular product is not fast enough or just to increase demand. Sponsored ads are keyword-targeted ads that put your ads across other search results (marked as sponsored) when a customer enters a particular search term. The costs are per click and you can set your own budget and track performance.

STEP 7: COMPLETE AND SELL YOUR PRODUCTS

The list of products offered for sale on the Amazon market and the management of your inventory are the most difficult aspects of selling at Amazon. Once a customer puts up an order, the next step is to take the product in hand.

Amazon offers two ways to make and ship the product:

Fulfillment by Merchant (FBM): As an Amazon supplier, you are responsible for inventory management, packaging, labeling and shipping products to specific customers.

Fulfillment by Amazon (FBA): Amazon stores and keeps your products in their fulfillment centers and handles the packaging and shipping of products to customers.

Execution by dealer (FBM)

Self-shipping is generally a good option for small sellers and those with lower profit margins. You can either calculate shipping costs or offer free shipping. The biggest upside of FBM is that you can keep everything in the house and not lose more profits on Amazon fees. The downside is that it's harder to qualify as an Amazon Prime sender if you're running an FBM. You can lose customers with premium accounts. The other disadvantage is that it's harder to get the Buy Box (more on that below) if you choose FBM.

If you find it difficult to process and send orders, select the shipping method Shipped by Amazon (FBA). With FBA, you can leverage Amazon's worldwide distribution centers, customer support, and other operational tools to grow your business faster than ever.

When you work with FBA, you store your inventory in Amazon distribution centers around the world. When a customer puts out an order, Amazon will pack and ship the product to the customer.

Here are some more benefits of using FBA:

Automatic Premium Entitlement: When you manage your products through Amazon FBA, your entire inventory automatically qualifies for Prime - an advantage that always causes customers to select your list first. At FBM, you must have a high volume and exceptional sales statistics to qualify as a premium seller.

Free Super Saver Permission: All products managed by FBA are eligible to receive free Super Saver for orders over $ 25. These lists have a better ranking on the Amazon site than the seller-filled lists.

A single inventory pool: With Amazon FBA, you can place orders not only on Amazon Marketplace, but also on your own e-commerce platform or on third-party websites. This gives you a seamless sales and mailing experience, no matter where you sell your product online.

Earn More Shopping Lists - Opting for FBA significantly increases your chances of winning when buying a particular product.

Superior ranking of products - Amazon favors FBA sellers in ranking products.

Apart from these advantages, the use of FBA has the advantage of being extremely simple. Instead of managing the logistics for order tracking and fulfillment, tracking, and handling customer service issues, simply send your inventory to Amazon and let the company manage the rest.

STEP 8: GET YOUR PROFITS

Amazon is a great way to increase the reach of your business, but selling through Amazon comes at a cost. Amazon deducts all charges from the proceeds of sale every two weeks. You will transfer the balance to your bank account every two weeks and will send you an e-mail notification each time you receive a new payment.

Here is a list of Amazon sales fees deducted from your sales:

Monthly Sales Fee - This is the fee you pay Amazon to access its market. Per seller pay $ 39.99 per month and retailers $ 0.99 per sale.

Referral Fees - These differ based on product category and size, but you typically do not need to pay more than 15% of the retail price of your product as a referral fee.

Returns Handling Fee - Amazon charges a refund handling fee for certain product categories.

Warehouse Removal Fee - This is a fee that charges Amazon FBA sellers who want Amazon to return or sell their unsold inventory.

Inventory Placement Fee - This is another fee charged by FBA sellers who want more control over the Amazon Order Processing Center that ships their inventory.

FBA Export Fees: At times, Amazon charges export fees for international shipping of products.

Collection and Collection Fee: Amazon charges a fee for picking up, packing, and shipping your products, as well as for handling customer service requests, based on the weight and size of your products. These charges may be $ 2.41 per product for smaller items, but may increase significantly for larger or larger items.

Monthly Inventory Fee: If you store your inventory in Amazon stores, you will receive a monthly charge based on the amount of storage space you use.

Although this list of fees seems overwhelming, a large number of independent sellers manage to make a good profit from selling on Amazon. The key to succeeding is the proper management of your inventory, lists of quality products and images, and fair prices for your products.

Here are some other relevant things to note as you start with your FBA Account:

Download your product list: To use FBA, download your product list in Seller Central. Proceed as with a product supplied by the seller. Then send all your inventory or parts inventory directly to Amazon, and take advantage of Amazon's reduced shipping fees.

Store and keep track of your inventory through Amazon: Amazon stores and manages your products in one or more of the more than 75 order fulfillment centers around the world. Of course you still have the inventory. You also have to pay storage fees for your items until they are sold.

Pay-per-Use: FBA has no minimum number of units. You will only pay for the number and weight of the units you store and actually send to customers. The only monthly fee is the monthly storage fee that allows you to use the Amazon distribution centers to store your products.

From Amazon picked up, packed and shipped: As soon as you receive an order, Amazon packages and sends your product directly to the customer.

Seamless Payment Management: Once the order has been shipped from Amazon, Amazon will collect the customer's payment, deduct the execution fee as a percentage of the total sale based on weight and number of items, and pay your bank account directly every 14 days.

Amazon Customer Service: If you use FBA, Amazon will serve as a direct contact to customer service.

FBA Charges

If you use FBA, you are responsible for two types of FBA charges:

Amazon Execution Fees: Amazon collects a fee for collecting, packaging, shipping, and managing customer service requests depending on the weight, volume and size of your products. These charges may be $ 2.41 per product for smaller items, but may increase significantly for larger or larger items.

Monthly Inventory Fee: If you store your inventory in Amazon stores, you will be charged a monthly fee depending on the amount of storage space you use.

The next step is a smaller additional BAF fee. Keep in mind that you'll have to pay a separate fee from all Amazon sellers, regardless of whether they use FBAs or not. We will discuss these in more detail later. For example, the benchmark fee calculated per product is typically not more than 15% of the quoted price. There is also the monthly subscription fee for pro sellers.

HOW TO SELL AT AMAZON: TIPS TO SUCCESSFULLY SELL PRODUCTS

There are several steps to selling your products on Amazon, and some are more complicated than others. However, if you take all these steps, you can take advantage of the incredible benefits of the Amazon platform and grow your business quickly.

How exactly can your small business benefit from selling on Amazon? Follow the following tips to make your Amazon product list stand out from the competition.

1. Check new orders daily

Since customer service is a key parameter that Amazon uses to determine your success as a salesperson, it is important to know when a new customer has purchased your product. In this way, you can quickly complete and send any order you receive.

Amazon will send you an email notification when you make a sale. However, these emails are not always reliable. To discover out how to sell on Amazon, you must consult the Seller Central portal daily. You can receive updates on new orders or notifications from your customers.

2. Confirm when you ship

Product vendors always have to confirm in the central vendor portal when an order has been shipped. Amazon will only debit your customer's credit card once the shipping has been confirmed. Alongside a good customer service, this step is important for you to pay quickly.

Remember that you must confirm the shipment within the time specified in your shipping settings. To verify that Amazon has shipped an order, click on the Orders tab and select the Confirm Shipment button.

3. Check your inventory regularly

You must be on top of your inventory at all times. Keep track of it. Realizing that you are out of stock and unable to fulfill a mission is a recipe for negative customer feedback that can significantly impact your future sales.

4. Keep the price information up to date

Buyers are most likely to pick the cheapest deals (assuming they're at the top of the results page). Therefore, if you sell or lower your prices, you must update your product lists to reflect these changes.

5. Optimize your ads

By selling on Amazon you enter a large market and become even bigger when it comes to search engines. Therefore, it is important to maximize your ads. You should make sure that you use all the available fields, SEO strategy and writing titles and descriptions when creating a list of products.

According to Aalap Shah, founder of the Digital Marketing Agency 1o8, "SEO is the best way to increase the visibility of the Amazon search engine when creating user-centered text and text." to convert the consumer. "

6. Respond quickly to customers

One of the benefits of selling to Amazon is your commitment to the brand's reliability and outstanding customer service. As a new vendor, you benefit from the credibility of Amazon. But it's up to you to maintain that credibility by being very reliable and listening to your customers.

For example, if an order is delayed, contact the customer to let him know. If a customer contacts you because he has not received a shipment or the product has been damaged, you can respond immediately and take the necessary action to remedy the situation.

7. Build a five-star rating

Maintaining good customer feedback is the key to your Amazon sales experience, both to improve buyer perceptions of your product listings and to position your products on the listings page.

Here are some tips you can use to get good feedback:

- Describe the products exactly and as detailed as possible
- Send products to customers as soon as possible.
- Contact customers proactively for information on delays or changes to their order
- Answer questions from customers within 24 hours
- Ask for positive customer feedback on your delivery notes

8. Win the box at Amazon

If you've already shopped at Amazon, you know that the platform allows multiple sellers to offer the same product. All sellers offering the same product can compete for the "Buy Box" for this product. In the shopping area of a product page, customers place items in their shopping cart.

By "winning" the shopping area, a seller becomes the default list for each product offered by multiple sellers. If you win this option, your sales will probably go up.

Amazon does not disclose the specific goals required for sellers to win the Buy Box. To increase the chances of winning this coveted spot, you should focus on optimizing your ads in the following four areas:

Price: Make sure your products are subject to competitive prices. The Buy Box Lists most often display the lowest available All-Inclusive rates, which is the total amount that the customer will pay, including postage.

Availability: Keep your favorite products always in stock and regularly update your warehouse numbers on the seller's portal.

Performance: Update your shipping settings in Seller Central to provide multiple shipping speeds and options, and if possible, free shipping.

Customer Service: Keep track of your customers 'comments and use the Account Integrity page in the Central Seller Performance section to monitor your customers' statistics.

Improving the position of your ad on the Amazon Quote List page requires testing, errors, and time. Work to give your customers a first-class experience and improve your logistics processes. Over time, these efforts will lead to more buy-box locations for your business and more customers.

9. Follow the instructions of the Amazon seller and understand the platform

This may seem like an obvious trick, but with a platform as big and prestigious as Amazon, it's more important than ever. Since all of the competition is sold through Amazon, Amazon does not tolerate sellers who do not follow their rules. Because of this, you want to be kept up to date with all of the Amazon salesperson policies and any changes. that are made for you. That way, you'll make sure you're in the best position to successfully sell on Amazon.

In addition to complying with Amazon's sales guidelines, it will also help you understand the platform as much as possible and develop a specific sales strategy from Amazon. According to Shannon Roddy, the creator of Marketplace Seller Racing, "success is not about a tactic or a simple trick, it's about an Amazon brand strategy: understanding how the Amazon platform works, Amazon thinks about it and how you can benefit from it while protecting your brand's capital (the perceived value of your products). "

How to sell services on Amazon

Currently, most retailers are aware of Amazon's impact on the product market and know that selling products at Amazon can be beneficial to their business.

However, if you're a service professional offering any kind of B2C service, you can also use Amazon to grow your business.

Amazon recently launched Amazon Home Services to provide Amazon customers with all sorts of professional services including bicycle mechanics, carpet cleaners, pet groomers and plumbers via the Amazon.com portal. The following are the types of professionals currently offering their services on Amazon. However, this list is growing steadily.

If you're a B2C service professional, you should know the following to begin selling at Amazon.

6 steps to sell services on Amazon

Think of Amazon Home Services (which we call AHS) as an Uber for B2C services: AHS enables Amazon customers to easily get a whole host of services by connecting to these service providers in their area. Visit the Amazon Home Services storefront store to learn how customers browse the services and what other service providers are currently involved in your neighborhood.

Would you like to become an Amazon service provider? Follow these six steps to apply for the program, set up your account, and connect with potential customers near you.

1. Apply for Amazon Home Services

Before you can register your professional services with AHS, you must complete an application form. To qualify for this program, you must comply with Amazon's essential requirements, including taking out liability insurance and providing a license for your transaction.

Then, Amazon does a background check of the business to make sure your business information is copy-content. All employees involved in home care services will also need to perform individual background checks.

If your request is received, you will receive an email from Amazon with an activation code and instructions for putting up your Amazon Home Service profile.

2. Set up your Amazon Home Services profile

Once you have been accepted as an Amazon service provider, you can create your storefront. This is the profile page where customers can learn more about your business.

You can write an introduction to your business, provide your service area by postal code, collect customer reviews, and more.

3. Create your packages

Amazon has created pre-packages for various categories of services based on the most frequent customer service requests (mainly product assembly and installation).

Once you have registered as a seller, you can choose one of these services to offer, set your prices, and specify the exact zip codes you'll be working in. Customers can order these packages at any time from Amazon.com. You will receive an e-mail notification when your new order is in the queue.

4. Use Seller Central

On the Amazon Seller Central portal, you can schedule online services, set up automatic communication with customers, manage your plans, pricing, payments, and more.

5. Create personalized services

Sometimes a customer near you is interested in a service installed in your wheelhouse that does not exactly match one of your predefined options. In this case, Amazon will provide custom service requests.

When a customer requests a personalized service, they will receive an email request and have 24 hours to bid. If the customer accepts the offer, you place the order as usual and Amazon takes over the entire processing of planning, billing and payment.

6. Payment received

Amazon Payments automatically manages payment for services sold through Amazon Home Services. You do not need to manage the billing or collection of your customers. Once you have completed an order, Amazon simply pays your income directly to your bank account. You should also understand that Amazon charges a percentage of the price of your service, which it deducts from your bank account each time you make a payment.

Amazon Home Service Fees

One of the main benefits of selling services on Amazon is that you do not pay in advance for leads or advertising. Since the fees are calculated as a percentage of sales, Amazon will only be paid if you do so.

For each service sold by Amazon on your behalf, the Company charges the following fees:

Transaction Fees: 5% of each transaction - includes billing, payment and fraud protection costs.

Platform Fee: About 10% to 20% of each transaction - covers marketing and advertising costs, vendor tools and customer service.

The total value of Amazon Home Services fees will depends on the price of your service and the type of service you provide:

Pre-built Services: Amazon will receive 20% of the Service Price portion up to $ 1,000 (5% transaction fee and 15% service platform fee) and 15% for the service price portion above $ 1,000 USD (5% transaction fee). and a 10% service platform fee).

Personalized Services: Custom Service Fees are 15% for the Service Price Share up to $ 1,000 (5% Transaction Fee and 10% Service Platform Fee) and 10% for the Service Price portion is higher than $ 1,000 (5%). Transaction and service platform fees of 5%).

Recurring Services: If a customer maintains a recurring service for your business (for example, physical workouts or monthly carpet cleaning services), Amazon will receive 10% of the service price for completed orders over $ 1,000 (this incurs 5% transaction fee and 5% service platform fee).

As you can see, Amazon collects all transaction and platform fees as a percentage of the price of the service, not as a lump sum. This percentage does not include taxes collected through Amazon's tax collection services.

SELLING ON AMAZON: TIPS FROM SUCCESSFUL SELLERS

Given all the steps, requirements, and techniques associated with selling to Amazon, it is always useful to hear the advice of real Amazon sellers. Here are some tips from business owners and experts on how to successfully sell on Amazon:

- Find your niche

"My first tip is to find your niche category where you can sell your unique products - do not enter a category that sells products everyone sells - it's important to take a look three or five years later to ensure that you are selling a certain high-quality product that suits a niche market, as competition keeps getting bigger, if your product is too broad, it will be lost in a sea of competitors selling the same and it will become one Race for the prize. "

- Jonathan Goldman, president and co-founder of Quantum Networks

"To be able to sell on Amazon, you must first find a place like a version of a high-end product at a modest price and create a recurring activity to ensure the customers return, it will honor you and allow you to Maximize the Lifetime Value of Each Customer Next, focus on the customer segments that can help you find your "ultimate goal" and use word of mouth. "

- Taylor Gilliam, Content Specialist, Webgility

Use attractive social ads and other external resources

"I firmly believe that social ads from platforms such as Pinterest and Facebook, which disrupt news feeds with engaging content (GIFs, videos, and other media), can help boost brand awareness and brand awareness. Lists and converts browsers into buyers "

- Aalap Shah, founder of the agency 1o8

"To get the most out of [selling on Amazon], you need to leverage the power of external sources like social media, influence marketing and blogging. Slowly adjust your budget accordingly. Contact the influencers in your industry and ask them if they are interested in reviewing your products and sending them a sample. "

- Ronald D'Souza, Director of Digital Marketing, Angel Jackets and Amazon Seller, Decrum

Find community support

"The best advice that can be given to someone who starts out is not to do it alone." Entering a community My business exploded when I started working with other sellers. "

-Ryan Reger, Author and owner of an e-commerce company

Do not forget your customers

"The customer is always right when selling on Amazon - take a loss if you have to."

-Yungi Chu, owner of an e-commerce company, HeadsetPlus.com

"Continue to value your customers and we love helping people do business."

-Seri Leong, co-founder of HighOh

The most important things to remember

Whether you're selling products or services, recognizing the Amazon brand and its logistical benefits is an incredible tool to grow your business that goes far beyond what you could probably achieve on your own. However, setting up your small business on Amazon takes time and attention.

And while the costs associated with selling on Amazon reduce your profit margins a bit (as is the case in most markets), you can offset those costs by developing a strategy: Decide how to optimize entries, promote your business, etc and work best on the seller's guidelines to sell successfully on Amazon.

Once you sign up for an Amazon seller account, the clock starts.

For your first monthly account fee after 30 days, you must honor all Amazon requirements from the first day.

Before you begin selling to Amazon, we recommend that you take each potential seller through several steps before you formalize the account registration process.

Required Documents (Checklist for Amazon Seller Account)

To complete the entire registration process for an Amazon seller account, you need a number of instant information, including:

1. Commercial Information.

Your company name, address and contact details

2. E-mail address.

An e-mail address that can be used for this company account. This e-mail account must already be configured because you will receive important e-mails from Amazon almost instantly.

3. Credit card.

An international credit card with a valid billing address. If the credit card number is not valid, Amazon will cancel your registration.

4. Telephone number.

A phone number where you can receive information during the registration process. Keep your phone ready when registering.

5. Tax number.

Your tax identity information, which may include your social security number or your company's tax identification number. To submit your tax identity data, the registration process makes a short detour via a "1099-K Tax Document Interview".

6. Tax ID information

#Tax ID information for the states in which you have a tax relationship. This physical presence is usually compromised by corporate offices, warehouses / 3PLs and call centers. In June 2018, the US Supreme Court revised this Law on the Liability of E-Commerce Providers to pay sales tax on online purchases.

I recommend you speak to a tax lawyer or accountant who deals in tax issues with online providers (such as salestaxandmore.com, catchingclouds.net, peisnerjohnson.com) or one of the transfer companies to get the latest information Amazon.

Questions that you need to have answers before creating your seller account

Some of the logistics required to become a successful seller should be resolved before setting up the seller account because you may not have enough time after the launch to resolve the issues.

1. Where do you want to send returns from Amazon orders?

As an Amazon salesman, it's imperative that you think about your return process.

Will you personally edit or return Amazon's returns to a company that specializes in testing/sorting returns and reselling the product (eg, tradeport.com, openboxreturns.com)?

2. Who in your team will handle Amazon customer requests?

The important thing is not only to have all the answers, but also to meet Amazon's requirements to answer all customer requests within 24 hours, regardless of the day of the year.

Therefore, before opening your Amazon Salesperson account, it is crucial to determine who (with a possible backup) is up to date.

3. If you want to use the Amazon Fulfillment by Amazon program, will you mix your products? Given the potential visibility for customers over 100 million Amazon Premium, I highly recommend the use of FBA. If you choose this path, you must decide whether you want to mix your products with the FBA inventory of other sellers of the same products.

Amazon offers this potentially lethal way for FBA sellers to send a product to Amazon distribution centers where they can mix with other FBA vendors' products. This can lead to confusion between your products and fake or inferior versions of what you are supposedly selling.

Unfortunately, you still have to explain to Amazon why a customer has complained about fake items when a mixed unit was selected to place an order on your account.

You need to fix this problem early because if you want to use FBA without the no sticker option, you'll need to activate your account to become a sticker FBA account before you create your first FBA shipping account on Amazon.

Although it is possible to become a glued account later, it can quickly become very complicated if you have already sent a product in FBA as a product without a sticker.

4. Are you planning to use a DBA name (company name) to use your Amazon seller account?

While some companies have legal reasons to use a different name for the customer, Amazon is also a place where many sellers deliberately hide their identity.

One reason for this is that brands do not want to know that they are selling online or that the brand is actually the reseller, and that they do not want their other retailers to know that they are selling products online directly to the consumers.

5. Have you checked if the products you want to list belong to categories managed by Amazon?

Amazon restricts the number of people who can sell in certain categories, and although the process of duplication is generally manageable, it is important to realize that you need to sign up to become one if the categories you want are gated.

Please visit the Amazon Approval Categories page before signing up to Amazon to learn more about the enforcement process and its application to your product categories.

6. Amazon has already begun targeting specific brands and article categories.

During your first 30 days or one month with a seller account, we advise that you add your entire planned catalog to your Amazon seller account. It does not take long to see if you have problems with specific brands and part numbers. You may need to revise your catalog or shut down your account if Amazon restricts the products to be sold.

Important knowledge and skills for Amazon providers

The Amazon market has its own rules and regulations, but also its own combination of skills that every salesperson should master quickly enough to be profitable and successful in the long term.

These include:

1. Stellar marketing content for creating product lists.

If the products you sell are already sold by others on Amazon, this is less important as you are likely to add your offer to the existing product list (you only need to specify the base price and quantity available) and the name of the SKU.

However, if your products are new to the Amazon catalog (you can easily check them by simply searching for your brand or UPC code in the Amazon.com search bar), you'll need to create content for fields such as product titles. , Chips, etc. product description and general keywords (to optimize the listing of your ads).

You also need product images for your ads. Visit the Amazon support page to add images for reference. However, it is recommended that sellers have multiple images, including a lifestyle image, if possible, to show the product being used.

This lifestyle image complements the main image with strict requirements, including a white background, no branding and at least 500 x 500 pixels.

2. A clear understanding of your product supply sources.

If your products sell really well on Amazon, do you know how to fill up fast enough to avoid long shortages?

If you specialize in fences and one-off purchases, you may not be able to easily re-create the same items, but you'll need well-defined processes to add new inventory as your Amazon cash flow improves. ,

3. A decision on whether you want to sell the same products over and over again.

In this case, you should use the Amazon in Seller Central replenishment alert tools, as well as other external forecasting tools such as the standalone options at www.forecastly.com, or the Inventory Management / Multi-Channel Control tools included in many integrated tools.

4. A process designed to identify and process expired stock.

Although everyone wants their products to be sold, in reality there will always be some who do not sell well and who need to be liquidated or sold through other channels to convert the stocks into working capital.

Amazon has tools that allow FBA sellers to identify outdated inventories, while non-FBA Amazon sellers need to track inventory by item number to determine what offers are needed for faster sales.

5. Understand the basic cost structure including overheads.

Too many salespeople at Amazon understand only the basics of business unit profitability and give a holistic view of the provider's overall profitability, rather than having a specific perspective on which field units determine what percentage to profit from while you are Understand which products actually cost money to be sold on Amazon.

Too many Amazon sellers do not know their profitability until the end of the year, when their accountant announced the final numbers, hoping to relieve the seller.

It is critical for sellers to understand and assemble all overheads and realize that these charges must be included in the total costs incurred by a seller to sell to Amazon.

6. Know who already sells the same items that you have at Amazon.

Amazingly, new sellers often join Amazon and list their products to determine that the new salesman can barely make sales or profit margins in their offers because of the level or type of competition.

Before creating an Amazon seller account, I strongly recommend that all vendors check their expected Amazon catalog to see if Amazon Retail is already selling these items.

If this is the matter, it is advised that you remove them immediately.

In addition, sellers should rate what prices are competitive on Amazon. If you find that you are rivaling with cheap competitors, this can be a good indication that it will be difficult for sellers to earn money in this category.

2. You know how long it takes for your ads to appear as Amazon sellers immediately after registering.

Amazon does not charge a new seller until the end of the first month at Amazon. During this time, the seller would have to create his product offers and activate at least a part of them with salable stock.

If you open your account and do not list your products, your professional seller account will be charged.

Knowing that feedback from the sale is important to Amazon to evaluate the performance of all new vendors, it is best that each new vendor to sign up for one of the many commenting tools. this sends a request for feedback to each customer.

These included:

- Feedbackgenius.com

- Feedbackfive.com

- Salesbacker.com

- Bqool.com

All of these can help a seller obtain customer feedback and show Amazon that his performance is satisfactory compared to his performance criteria while maintaining customer satisfaction.

From there you want to get to know certain tactics of Amazon, such as:

Win the box.

Determine your sales strategy (eg retail arbitrage).

Choose the right products.

Maximize your profits with the Amazon Inventory Management System

Amazon has fundamentally changed the online retail marketing game for Amazon sellers. Many of them have not yet explored the e-commerce website online and they have already reached the first choice for merchants and shoppers when shopping online. To accomplish this in such a short time, Amazon has made every effort to reach the top with some features like the Amazon Inventory Management System.

Warehousing is the most important requirement. Amazon has the world's first online e-commerce portal. Any merchant that does not meet this requirement will be blacklisted by Amazon, which can be a nightmare as no-one should miss participating in the global shopping revolution.

Since Amazon makes it easy, the only way to relieve traders is to offer Fulfillment By Amazon (maybe a bad joke). However, once you know more about FBA, trading with Amazon will certainly be an entertaining task. Fulfillment By Amazon is a great installation provided by Amazon in all stores.

It aims to manage your inventory, branding and packaging, shipping and delivery, which can be very stressful if you are a foreign reseller on Amazon.

How does Amazon's inventory management really help?

In addition to smoothing the relationship between you and Amazon, this also helps increase your revenue. Your timely delivery and your entire stock lead to positive reviews and easy exchange. Always avoid signs of rush and short-term inventory of your products. Customer feedback is difficult to obtain but with the right professional attitude you can get these comments.

Every positive opinion counts in a new Amazon market. Stock availability is also guaranteed.

What is Amazon Inventory Management?

The warehouse management of Amazon is FBA. Several tools are available today on the market to aid you to manage FBA and make your work more comfortable. It helps you maintain your inventory and deliver your items to all markets.

Amazon Inventory Start

Before you start FBA, you must create an account with Amazon Seller Central or Vendor Central. The FBA option is reserved for users who use the central provider because the central Amazon provider is an established brand. Once you've set up a central platform for vendors, choosing FBA is a good idea if you want to take good advantage of the new Amazon. Here are some basic starting steps:

• Add FBA to your account.

• List your products: you can do this manually or have your inventory management software do it for you. Add your products one after the other or in bulk to the Amazon catalog.

• Keep your products operational: In addition to manufacturing, you must have your product ready for shipping and delivery. It is important that the product is delivered to the customer intact and excellently. Shipping and packaging materials are also available on Amazon under shipping and preparation materials. It will be delivered to your address. You can also order basic materials such as cardboard and bubble wrap.

• Send to Amazon: Select the appropriate couriers and carriers and ship the shipment to Amazon distribution centers. You can use tools to track your inventories and make sure they arrive on time in the warehouse. Once they are stored at Amazon, your stress is over.

• Order, pack and ship items: Most orders on Amazon are shipped for free, and Amazon Prime customers get an extra bonus on fast and free shipping. Once the customer has ordered the same, the product is selected from the warehouse, carefully packaged for delivery, and then shipped to the customer. With Amazon Inventory Management best practices, the product can be quickly accessed, sorted, and delivered.

This procedure also allows the customer to receive regular updates of their order by following them with the help of the code. It serves both the fact that the customer is at home, ready to receive the order, as well as the pleasure he feels when his order has finally arrived at the door.

• Backoffice customer support: The work is not finished here. Even after selling and transferring money, Amazon is trying to maintain its relationship with the customer.

In addition to shipping, FBA also offers back-office customer service. These services apply to all products sold on Amazon. The customer service team will assist the customer with a refund, return, follow-up, and other similar requests regarding our product. This service is available all year round. As a global franchise company, it's available around the clock and throughout the week.

Does Amazon FBA affect only registered retailers of Amazon?

No. This shipping and packaging facility is an exclusive facility. This means that you do not want to sell your items on Amazon's retail platform, but only want to use the fulfillment feature. You can do this with Amazon. , As a unique feature, the FBA can act as a logistics service provider.

In addition to those who want to sell on Amazon but do not want to use their FBA, this option is also available. You can choose to sell only your items on Amazon. However, use a third party to ship and package your product. In either case, you have the option to choose exactly the facilities that you would choose Amazon for.

For example, if you're a local retailer looking to take advantage of Amazon's large retail platform, you can only sell on Amazon. If you are a foreign reseller of Amazon, but trade with another retail platform, but intend to use FBA, this option is also available.

However, it is often found that customers typically have more confidence in "sold and shipped from Amazon" than in other private companies. So you definitely want to benefit from Amazon. In addition, dealers who use FBA also benefit from urgent one-day orders for gift wrappers and on-time delivery services.

Would there be a mismanagement of the stock?

Although Amazon is a well-known brand in the US and Asia, it still has its roots. Given that it needs to start from scratch, many local and small retailers fear that their products will be lost if they believe that Amazon is a large retail market that handles multiple products simultaneously.

However, this is a legitimate concern; Even a small difference in product loss during the transaction or late delivery impact new merchants. Well, there is nothing to worry about. Amazon uses the latest technology to keep track of products until they are successfully sent to the customer. In addition, the dealer is kept up to date.

In addition, for the simplest management of Amazon Inventory, special tools are available on the market designed specifically for asset management. These tools help you manage product distribution, packaging, pricing, delivery and many other details about the retail market.

Amazon Warehouse Management System

The Amazon department store is a huge department store. Even if the products have been misplaced, they can be tracked based on the previous scan. The worker on the ground is then asked to access the product as soon as possible. Timely delivery is therefore essential, as time is of the essence for Amazon sellers.

Amazon FBA Price of the seller

The pricing structure of the FBA is very flexible and facilitates competition. The less you pay for the FBA, the more you can focus on revising the prices of your products. In addition to low prices, FBA also offers many other benefits, including free shipping, improved product visibility and other premium customer service.

FBA's services also include storing your inventory in Amazon distribution centers, customer service, product returns, pricing, and packaging orders.

In the past, Amazon had a different fee structure for the holiday season from October to December, but now that the directive has been amended, they have the same fee structure throughout the year. This also applies to Amazon Australia, which has just been launched.

The last changes to the FBA pricing structure were implemented on February 22, 2018 and are valid for the whole year. The fees are based on the volume weight (length x width x height in inches) divided by 339, which was 166 previously.

This only applies to large standard items weighing more than one pound. This dimension weight is also calculated for multi-channel execution and inventory placement.

A fully-managed sizing site is available on the Amazon site and can be used as a reference. It should also be noted that these little changes apply to a product that left the Amazon Processing Center after February 22, 2017. Shipments delivered before this date will be subject to earlier charges.

How can you improve your Amazon Inventory Management techniques?

Well, here are some wisdom nuggets to help you manage your Amazon inventory so that you can enjoy the Amazon FBA process to the full.

- Use the AITS (Amazon Inventory Tracking software)

As you grow and learn with Amazon, so do your inventory and manufacturing. Handling a large inventory can be a tedious and tedious task. Excel spreadsheets and physical documents are a thing of the past. There is a very advanced inventory management software that makes it easier for you to negotiate with Amazon.

The Amazon Inventory Tracking software makes sure you save just enough. no more and no less. You will also receive notification of manufacture, packaging and price changes. The tools built into the software guide you through the process and facilitate transactions. Retailers often experience radically positive growth in inventory management software trading.

The warehouse monitoring and control software also stores sales and profitability data. With pricing and revenue anchored in the software, you can also keep track of your profits and send you notices on a daily, monthly, and quarterly basis whenever you need them. Based on these custom data, you can plan your strategies.

• Be prepared for seasonal sales fluctuations: the holiday season is the perfect time to sell and work harder as a shopkeeper. You have to keep up and make sure the seasonal gap between supply and demand is not too big.

Make sure your inventory is well-stocked, as no one wants to have the "Out of Stock" ad when he buys his loved ones for Christmas. In addition, do not store too many products that could result in higher storage, packaging and packaging costs.

The seasonal sale does not apply to all products. Some products sell more while others sell less. So you have to choose which of your products will make the most sales while selling less, and store your inventory accordingly. Keep your supplier up to date and note that delivery times may be due to weather conditions or storage issues. However, keep these factors in mind when storing items in your warehouse.

• Know Your Exact Participation Rate in Amazon Inventory: This is the exact percentage of your investment in Amazon Inventory sales. This is the speed with which they are sold in the inventory. With this estimate, you get to know the inventory. This helps to avoid overstocking or understocking and thus maintain a good balance.

The standard stock rate is three months. You should have enough stocks at a time, which would take at least three months since you trade worldwide. The weather plays an important role in transportation and you do not want it to bother you. For this reason, a comfortable storage rate is of the utmost importance.

The Amazon Inventory software can do the calculation for you, calculate daily sales trends and reflect the exact inventory rate for you.

• Slow down when needed: A good sales strategy is not to reach the maximum number of customers, but to lose a customer. Sometimes your sales exceed expectations and reach a higher than expected level due to exceptional marketing or re-rating techniques.

This leads to the exhaustion of your inventory. If you exhaust all of your warehousing products and are unable to meet the supply and demand cycle, there may be negative corrections due to delivery delays or "non-inventory". You can finish your inventory sooner than expected, but this will certainly lead to a cascade effect or your future sales.

How to slow sales down

To prevent this from happening, you can slow down the development by permanently ending your marketing strategy or by upgrading the product to a slightly higher rate. In this way, you will not necessarily lose customers, but will temporarily slow down your sales to keep your brand long term. If you reduce the speed, you also have time to replenish your inventory to get back into the game. Another method is to limit promotional offers to a limited inventory in order to attract attention. Then you can revoke the action as soon as the turnover reaches the magic number. One of the methods for promotions is to offer free items, free shipping, etc.

Do not forget that Amazon needs about four hours to finish the action after you press the stop button to make sure you have enough time to manage the four hours since you want to be dissatisfied by your customer's Comments noticed. A method can also take longer shipping dates, but this is not really relevant for the customer.

Know the supply chain and lead time

It is about knowing the supply chain from the time of the first delivery of the product to its arrival in the warehouse. This is the amount of time it takes for the product to reach the customer once it is commanded. When you understand these facets, you get to know the transport system and, if possible, try to reduce some tedious activities.

You know, it is important to know who, when, how, where and when in the transport system and as a dealer. It is important to maintain this supply chain smoothly, especially in a new market like Amazon. It also helps you plan your unforeseen scenario and prepare for the worst-case scenario. As mentioned above, it is advised that you always have a stock of three months in your inventory.

• An alternative to Inventory: As an Amazon reseller, you have the option of making a direct shipment by asking the manufacturer or wholesaler to take care of your shipment and its packaging. Every time you make a sale, you do not have to worry about shipping or storage because the manufacturer manages this directly. This also simplifies the storage fee for you. When you design strategies to increase sales, the product is sent from the manufacturer to the customer.

This completely eliminates the stress of Amazon FBA or Amazon Inventory. However, you must make sure that the product is shipped on time and without delay, as this may lead to negative ratings. In addition, you do not want a customer annoyed by the "Out of Stock" sign.

If an error in direct delivery to Amazon Australia led to negative results, you could even be blacklisted. In addition, it could be sold on Amazon, but it would appear as "sold by XYZ and shipped by ABC," which clearly shows no link between you, the merchant, and Amazon. In addition, this may increase the price of your product as the merchant now charges additional shipping and storage costs. So it's a risky decision to make a direct delivery, but you still have to weigh the benefits and cons before coming to a conclusion.

Dropship also makes it easy to load lists and manage Amazon software for inventory management.

Increase your sales with the Amazon Seller app

To conclude, Amazon has built its online presence based solely on customer satisfaction and on-time delivery. Without proper management of Amazon Inventory this would not have been possible. As long as the merchants do not maintain the Amazon FBA inventory, the transaction will not be completed.

Amazon uses the best mechanism to deliver its services. As an Amazon partner, you should also take advantage of Amazon Inventory Process best practices. Selling on Amazon is usually very rewarding, but it's not an easy task, especially once you sell by volume. Your inventory increases as your orders increase. To succeed, you must have a strong asset management strategy.

This part of the book introduces seven tips for improving your Amazon inventory management. But let's first explain why good inventory management is so important to Amazon sellers.

Why inventory management is important to Amazon providers

Here are the main reasons why it's important to take control of your Amazon inventory:

Attracting buyers and making sales - When you run out of stock, your customers are buying your competitors.

Reduce Warehousing - If you have too much stock, your money will be stored in unsold goods and additional storage costs.

Reduce inventory footprints - Keeping track of your inventory levels can help you reduce losses from poorly managed storage, receiving bugs, and stealing employees.

Reduce waste - When you sell perishable items, inventory management helps you track expiration dates and avoid losses from damaged or unsaleable products. Nearly half of the small businesses do not have a good inventory management system, but it's easy to control your Amazon inventory more closely. Here is how.

7 Tips for Improving Amazon Inventory Management

1. Use the Amazon Inventory Management Software

Manually tracking your inventory in documents or spreadsheets is time-consuming and error-prone. Inventory monitoring software is one of the best ways to automate your inventory management tasks and ensure that you have enough inventory throughout the year. Retailers often see an increase in inventory efficiency of nearly 40% through the use of warehouse management software.

The Amazon Seller Central Dashboard shown below includes a number of built-in tools that you can access for free.

In the Dashboard, Amazon Selling Coach publishes key inventory data to help sellers track inventory and purchase requirements. By monitoring your sales and inventory trends, Amazon warehouse management tools can help you determine how many items are sold to Amazon daily, weekly, and monthly. You can then draw trends to determine the inventory required for products over different time periods. This comprehensive review of your sales and inventory trends is essential for making smart purchasing decisions.

2. Understand your inventory turnover rate

The speed at which you sell through your Amazon inventory is generally referred to as your inventory turnover rate. To determine your inventory turnover rate, on average, you should know how fast your products are selling to Amazon. With this piece of information, you can calculate how much inventory you need to order to maintain inventory between inventory shipments. This will also aid you to avoid excessive or inadequate purchases when reordering.

In general, Amazon sellers who import goods are targeting a 3-month inventory turnover rate, meaning they plan to sell through a warehouse order within 3 months. A better way to predict inventory turnover and replenishment needs is to use a forecasting tool to track the daily sales trends for your products. Amazon's Amazon Selling Coach, an integrated inventory forecasting tool, tracks sales based on your inventory availability and recommends the quantities required for order fulfillment over a period of time, through your supplier's dashboard.

3. Understand the time in your supply chain

Your supply chain refers to the movement of inventory from initial delivery to arrival in your warehouse. The delivery time is the time it takes for the stock to arrive when ordering. By understanding your supply chain and schedules, you can identify who, what, where, and when to participate in finding, receiving, and storing your Amazon inventory.

To keep your supply chain functioning properly, keep an eye on your vendor's manufacturing and scheduling plans and plan to overcome worst-case scenarios. This is especially important if you use foreign suppliers, as shipping delays can take weeks. Make sure you keep stocks in reserve to cover unforeseen delays in your supply chain when you buy goods overseas.

4. Schedule inventory with seasonal fluctuations in sales in mind

Seasonal demand and holiday purchases impact inventory levels as customer demand increases and delivery times are extended. It is important to know which products are fast at specific seasons and which products are slow.

It is important that you plan your inventory at least two months in advance. You want to increase the quantity of products ordered that are in high demand during peak sales periods and reduce your orders for off-season products.

It is also important to consider the long delivery times for stocks ordered in high season. In this way, you can place orders with a sufficient lead time for delays due to seasonal demand and other factors such as the weather. By maintaining open communication with your suppliers, you can also avoid unplanned delays and late deliveries.

5. Consider a direct delivery instead of stock.

For direct delivery, the manufacturer of your product manages the inventory and ships the goods directly to your customers on your behalf when you make a sale. Direct delivery is less risky because you do not have to buy inventory that may not be sold. Also, you do not have to pay for storage when shipping directly.

It is important that you choose your direct mailers wisely so that you are profitable in the end. Many charge additional fees, which increases the cost of the goods compared to the usual profit margin. Also, make sure your shipping service provider is Amazon-compatible. They must be shipped as promised and report inventory so you do not sell out-of-stock items.

Because direct delivery orders are not directly controlled by the seller, Amazon has strict direct delivery policies. If this is not followed exactly, your seller account may be suspended.

6. Be strategic in promotions and sales

Promotions such as retail prices or free shipping offers boost your Amazon business. However, an increase in sales due to a great promotion may deplete your inventory before your next delivery, leaving you behind with belated orders, angry customers, and a lower-ranking on Amazon.

One solution is to set a threshold for a defined number of items that will be promoted in your inventory. Once this number is reached, you can remove the action and sell the remainder at a higher price so as not to exhaust yourself.

If you plan to sell completely, you must set a threshold that covers four hours of promotional sales. This number can be found in Seller Central. Four hours is the key here, as it takes Amazon up to four hours to clear a promotion after stopping it. This will give you enough inventory to cover the sales that will be made as soon as you finish the action.

Another way to make a promotion is to order your supplier a reserve of promotional items with a future shipping date. If your promotion is successful and you need a fast shipping, you can contact the supplier to change the shipping date. However, if the action is too late, you can cancel or extend the shipment date of the replenishment order to avoid over-ordering.

7. If necessary, slow down the demand for your inventory

Good Advertising Amazon can get your products out of stock, which is a great thing. However, if you can not meet buyers' demands with a sufficient supply, you run the risk of losing customers to your competitors and facing a lower ranking on Amazon.

If you observe that you are out of stock during a promotion or at any point in time, you should increase your prices and discontinue an ad campaign to curb demand. These measures can slow your sales in the short term, but it is better not to reach inventory levels over a longer period of time.

It takes time to gain a good reputation as an Amazon salesman, and you can not afford to lose your reputation or your hard-earned rank due to poor inventory management. Follow the tips above to keep your inventory at a reasonable level and stay competitive at Amazon.

FILLING THE FBA INVENTORY

In general, Amazon sellers are so focused on finding new products on Amazon that they often forget to maximize the profitability of their existing product package.

It's easier to increase your company's profits through proper inventory management than doing research on new products. Effective inventory management ensures that you do not miss any products that you want to sell when customers want to buy, and that your money is properly invested in the right products so you can transfer your inventory to earn profits.

Below is a discussion with Jeremy Biron, founder of Forecastly, the main difficulties that Amazon sellers face in restocking FBA, including supply chain management and stockpile prevention.

Question: Why did you decide to create an inventory management tool?

My experience is e-commerce and internet marketing, with a particular interest in the Amazon market. We created the internal software about 3 years ago. We wanted to do the FBA refill correctly.

I've seen what kind of software is available on the market, and when I completed warehouse management training, I also found major shortcomings in the management of FBA inventories in terms of restructuring and inventory levels.

That's why I chose Forecastly about a year ago, after receiving the same comments from other Amazon providers. Shortly thereafter, we had our first sellers on the platform.

Q. What are the biggest challenges in replenishing FBA inventories?

1) Calculation of the sales speed:

Many of the seller's problems (at the time the company was founded) concerned the wrong calculation of sales speed. Since then, some applications have resolved this issue, which is a good thing - but it was an integral part of our decision to start the business.

If a product is out of stock or unavailable for half a month and you sell 100 units, the situation is very different if you sell 100 units and the product is in stock because your sales speed should be double that. she was.

If you do not correct this at the beginning of the process, the other failed calculations that you perform after that moment are irrelevant. This is the beginning of the refilling process. If this is not the case, then everything that will follow is flawed after that time.

2) Integrate the turnaround time:

Another important element of inventory management is the precise integration of deadlines. For a large number of applications, deadlines are not adequately taken into account - this is the time of stocks.

Assuming that your processing time is 30 days and 45 days, you are very likely to have a stock of 15 days, which can be very expensive for a seller.

According to Forecastly, "vendors often underestimate the impact of an out-of-date FBA on an Amazon company, and you obviously run out of product sales if you do not have stock in stock, which is the most obvious problem, but you do not have to stock the impact of an event is to take into account your inventory forecasts in the future. "

"Sellers often underestimate their forecasts when an item has recently sold out, a problem that amplifies when the Out of Stock event has occurred over an extended period of time.

3) Anticipate top sales:

The other challenge is to accurately predict the likelihood of revenue growth. If you can predict a peak, you can probably reduce the risk of shortages.

An increase in sales could include external factors such as promotions and seasonality. These are two elements that are difficult to integrate into your forecasts and that you can not easily identify in an Excel spreadsheet (where many salespeople calculate their stock levels).

Excel works very well if you are a small seller. However, if you want to do it properly on a large scale, you need to be able to accurately predict those peaks and include those external factors in your forecasts.

This is mainly due to the seasonality of the Amazon, which refers to the category level for a certain period of the year. Sellers should also be aware of the impact of advertising. For example, if you give 100 units at a 50% discount because you want to stimulate the sale, you can not assume that the sales speed of 100 units will persist after you stop giving units at 50%.

Inventory management is about a lot of "secret sauce". You do not have to know exactly how this works, but as a seller, you need to know what's included in your equation, including seasonality and / or promotions. The same sold out for days. It's important to know what the system does, but not necessarily how it does it.

It is very important that sellers ask themselves if they think it pays to send their suppliers and their costs directly to Amazon.

I do not think the Amazon refill tool works as well as some other tools available on the market, though at the same time, it may also be beneficial for some smaller vendors - a starting point.

1. You can not just rely on Amazon

Although Amazon FBA provides you with some inventory management tools, it is assumed that you have a stock of your self-stored products. However, as more and more vendors use Amazon FBA or other alternative execution methods, such as the purchase of dropshipping, this is becoming increasingly rare. Even then, Amazon will notify you (at the most) a few weeks later, and there is not always enough time to refill.

How can you be proactive in this regard? By knowing your sales speed and delivery cycle. The easiest way to do that is by not just relying on the tools provided by Amazon. If you invest in FBA management software, rather than relying on the Amazon-powered dashboard, you can set up your own resupply notifications and keep your inventory up-to-date.

This will ensure that you do not disappoint your customers with overdue orders or excessive sales.

2. Pay attention to every product

All your products are unique - and you have to treat them that way. It's easy to consolidate orders and save costs and shipping costs. However, this will not benefit you if half of your inventory stays on the shelves and does not sell like the other half. This means that you have to examine each product individually and order the stocks accordingly. Of course, the best artists have to be reorganized more frequently, while your slow actions should only be bought when they move.

It can be beneficial to automate the sales cycles of some of your products once you have an idea of their performance. Make sure that you also take into account the latest trends and the current situation: Seasonal sales waves can have a big impact on how much inventory you need.

3. Keep an eye on your promotions

Actions are a great way to increase sales, generate ratings, and improve your ranking on Amazon. But you have to monitor them.

Of course, you want your promotions to work well. However, if they work too well, serious inventory issues can occur. If they are too successful, it can significantly reduce your profit margins (much more than expected). The worst case is the unexpected failure. In that case, all the work you have done with promotion to improve your rankings was useless. Not only will you lose potential sales, but you will also reduce your ranking and have an additional deficit in the beginning.

To counter unsuccessful promotions, you can create a protected inventory from your inventory in the Seller Central section of Amazon by placing an order for yourself. You can keep the inventory for two weeks. So, if you find that your promotion is starting and your inventory is low, you can stop the action and cancel the order as this inventory is automatically offered for sale.

4. If you have concerns, keep an extra reserve

You may have heard of Just-in-Time Inventory Management, which does not keep inventory but only orders for sale. This approach is ideal for controlling inventory and reducing costs. But for Amazon salespeople, keeping stock levels that way while keeping customers satisfied is very difficult. You need to closely monitor your inventory and know the exact periods of increased demand.

For this reason, it makes sense to reserve part of your budget to provide additional reserve when needed. This can be done through additional products that keep you ready, cost you inventory, or reserve extra space in your warehouse. Emergency Planning helps you prepare for when things are not going as planned - what you need to sell successfully on Amazon.

Need more advice from Amazon? Here are common mistakes to avoid in Amazon inventory and tips for reducing long-term storage costs for Amazon FBA.

Whether you're new to the Amazon market or a seasoned salesman, you're certainly making mistakes along the way. Some manufacturer errors can cost time and money, while others prohibit selling to Amazon, such as the wrong inventory management on Amazon.

Common Errors that Sellers make

The ten most common errors committed by Amazon sellers are the following. Try to avoid them at all costs.

1. Wrong prices and stock quantities

The lists and quantities available on Amazon are put online almost immediately. New sellers have no opportunity to practice before. Make sure you list your inventory carefully.

If you have no inventory, enter zero. If you have stocks, specify the quantity exactly.

It is also important that your prices are listed correctly. It happened that sellers accidentally came in for a very low price and that their products sold quickly, which cost them thousands of dollars. Using Amazon Inventory Automatic Inventory Sync Software is the best way to manage Amazon Inventory Management.

2. Descriptions of elements that do not match

Amazon makes it easy to match existing product lists with the product you sell. Do not forget to be very careful when doing this. You need to make sure your ad portrays exactly what you sell. If your customers receive products that are almost identical to those in your ad, they can complain and you can be suspended if your ad does not match the right product.

3. Ignore policy changes

If you receive an email or other notification that Amazon has changed a policy, do not search it and press the Delete key. It is essential that you read it vigorously and check that the changes are correct for you. Reading takes only a few minutes, and most changes are minor. As a result, compliance usually does not take long. This can prevent you from being paused or terminated.

4. No clear return policy

It is inevitable that a customer wants to return a product at a certain time. It is important that you clearly specify your return policy so buyers can be informed and make an informed decision before purchasing. You do not want to interact with your customer, resulting in a complaint or negative feedback.

5. Do not collect comments

Amazon's Supplier Performance and Product Quality department oversees seller feedback for each sale, quality (rank), and quantity (typically receiving about 5 percent of sales feedback). If you are low in one category or another, your account may be suspended. You may want to think about a vendor who will assist you in applying for feedback - there are several, including Feedback Genius and FeedbackFive.

6. Does not respond quickly to customers

When an Amazon customer sends you a request, you have 24 hours to respond, whether it's a weekend or a public holiday. If you do not respond to the customer's request within the given time, you will be notified by Amazon. If this happens too often, your account may be suspended.

Respond quickly to requests for information, even if the request or problem can not be resolved immediately.

7. Performance error

If you are a new salesman and execute your own order, it is easy to make mistakes. Maybe the delivery of an order has been delayed a bit. You may forget to share tracking information with Amazon, or you may feel that you are no longer up-to-date and need to cancel an order.

It is important that you master your order from the beginning. You may want to consider the Fulfillment by Amazon program if you are considering automated transfers or both.

8. Do not use the right tools

As an Amazon seller you just can not do it all by yourself. There are various tools you can adopt to make your business smoother. As discussed above, you can use an Amazon Inventory Management software solution. Do not try to do everything yourself. Find the right tools to help you.

9. Competing against Amazon

Before purchasing or listing an inventory on Amazon, check whether Amazon Retail sells the products. The fight against Amazon Retail is likely to be a losing battle as it manages its own capability to win the sale, sometimes even at a loss. You can check Keepa.com to see if the product you want to sell is already on Amazon Retail and list it accordingly.

10. Be contented

It can be easy to stop checking on and analyzing your company's status and indicators, especially if everything is alright. However, as it often takes some time for differences to occur, it is important to stay informed, even if your business is successful. This helps you to take advantage of trends and edit areas that need to be improved long before they become a problem.

Inventory Management Amazon requires a lot of experimentation: see what works and what does not, then make adjustments. However, if you know some of the common mistakes, you can avoid major disasters. To understand Amazon's inventory management, you need to stay up-to-date, sell quality products, provide great customer service, and get to know your business.

Fulfillment By Amazon (FBA) suppliers may not be aware of Amazon's long-term FBA storage fees for products that have been placed on Amazon shelves for more than a year.

According to Amazon, products that are either stored or stored too long in their warehouses limit the ability to make room for fast-selling, low-cost products.

For example, Amazon cleans up inventory on the 15th of each month and rates the so-called "long-term storage costs" for its BAF customers whose inventories were stored too long in their data centers. Commands.

How much does FBA long-term storage cost from Amazon?

It depends on what you have in stock. Amazon charges you the highest of two scenarios:

In space: $ 6.90 per cubic foot for inventories stored for more than 12 months

Per unit: $ 0.15 per storage unit stored for more than 12 months.

Depending on what you sell, Amazon will calculate your costs based on the two scenarios above and charge you the highest amount.

Yes, it's a bit hard to understand. For example, suppose you sell small key chains and have about 100 in an FBA warehouse. You may not need much space, say a cubic foot. If you do not sell these key fobs and store them on the Amazon shelves for 365 days, Amazon will charge your fees:

  Per room: $ 6.90, as your key fobs occupy one cubic foot of their warehouse.

Per unit: $ 15, as you have 100 key fobs, each costing $ 0.15.

Amazon will charge you $ 15, as this is the highest value.

How to avoid long-term storage costs

Now is a great time to consider what you can do to avoid Amazon's long-term FBA storage costs.

- Check the status of your inventory

The first step is to determine the status of your inventory and determine if you might have to pay a fee. If you have FBA inventory management software, such as: For example, the solution offered by Ecomdash allows you to generate reports and use calculator tools that tell you what you need to know. Otherwise, you can access the Amazon Inventory Health status report to see if any inventory was stored too long in Amazon distribution centers.

- Determine how risk assets should be managed

Once you identify the vulnerable inventory, you must propose a strategy to avoid long-term storage costs. You have a few options:

- Request the distance

It's the easiest option. If you submit a removal request, Amazon will return your requested inventory to your company for a small fee. The return shipping cost can be up to $ 0.50 per unit, oversized products only $ 0.60 per unit. This may be the most trustworthy way to avoid long-term storage costs as long as you can afford to meet your margins.

- Application for removal

Your second option is to file a cancellation request. For a price that is below the payout price, Amazon keeps the stock for you. Choosing this option can be difficult. However, if the amount you have paid for your inventory is minimal, it may be the best. Maybe you've tested a new product that has not sold, so it's time to cut the bait.

Unfortunately, you will be charged a fee even if you choose Amazon for your inventory. The exclusion is $ 0.15 for standard size units and $ 0.30 for oversize units. The good thing about the elimination is that Amazon really makes things easier. All you have to do is choose to remove the products and Amazon will do the rest.

- Try to sell the items

Their third option is to try to sell the inventory at risk before Amazon rates the long-term storage costs. This is the best option for you if there is a chance you can sell your products even with a low-profit margin. There are several methods to do this:

Create a Sales Action - With Amazon, you can easily add actions to your products. Go to the Vendor Central section of the Amazon website for the Advertising drop-down menu and select Promotions. From there, you can offer your customers free shipping, one buy, one receive, receive money or other offers. In this way, you may be able to move at least part of your inventory, making the cost of removal or disposal more acceptable.

Creating a Promoted Product Campaign - If you believe your inventory has remained on shelves because customers are having trouble finding it, then you're bidding on Amazon sponsored products. They bid on relevant keywords. If your bid wins, your ad will be shown to the customer. It's a kind of pay-per-click, meaning you only pay when someone clicks on your message. If it works, your products will be much more visible and part of your inventory could be sold. Here are some tips for optimizing your Amazon ads.

The biggest benefit of placing your orders with Amazon is that you do not have to worry about everything that happens between sending your inventory to Amazon and returning it to potential customers. The steps between these two tasks, such as order processing, packaging, shipping and delivery, are supported by Amazon. Easy to see why it is beneficial?

Distributors have been around for some time - retailers rely on the company's warehouses and deliveries, while retailers charge retailers using volume discounts. FBA is a bit different, Amazon is a market, they have an active interest in making the products sell well on their website. There is an added benefit of not having to look for your customers.

The benefits of using FBA are threefold, as we have stated in previous chapters:

Imagine scenario 1, where you are a regular seller at Amazon, and scenario 2, where you are an FBA seller. Most FBA products and Amazon Prime can be delivered at very low prices. Customers who need a product immediately will always choose FBA instead of a regular seller. While a Scenario 1 vendor needs to add a shipping fee to its product price, Scenario 2 vendors can increase the price of the competition, despite the fees charged by Amazon, and thereby achieve a higher payment.

Amazon products can be purchased and delivered 24 hours a day, 7 days a week. Once you have sent your products to the

Amazon warehouse, you have nothing left to do. We talk less about work and yet more visibility.

About 50% of Amazon customers prefer FBA. They know that Amazon manages their product and it will arrive sooner. In addition, the same customers are even willing to pay more for the same article to be sent by Amazon than for a third party seller.

Even if you're a small retailer, you can start selling at Amazon without worrying about many aspects of online sales. One aspect you should consider is the quality of the product. Regardless of the manufacturer of your product, you can not easily receive the shipment of the product and send it to Amazon as it is. You should always have your own quality control to make sure all the products you send are in a salable condition, reducing your chances of a return.

How do you save an inventory that you can not see? Warehouse management is always a sensitive issue for most retailers, and all the more so if any additional space you use in the warehouse will incur additional costs. On the one hand, your vendor's bill goes down when your stock runs low, and on the other hand, if you store too much, your money gets stuck in the inventory. If you sell multiple products through FBA and each has a different delivery time, you should independently monitor sales and replenishment for each product. It may be intimidating, but very effective.

The following should be noted if you want to become an FBA seller:

The cost of storage and shipping is prohibitive for you when considering an FBA.

The fact that Amazon is a market does not stop you from finding buyers.

If Amazon customers choose between third-party products and FBA products, they prefer FBA and are willing to pay higher fees.

If you sell multiple products through FBA that are sourced from multiple manufacturers, you must consider the inventory of each product separately.

If products remain in an Amazon warehouse for longer than a specified period, additional fees may apply.

Identify and Set Prices for Your Products for FBA

The basis of arbitrage is that as a retailer you buy products from a cheaper source and sell them at a higher price. In most cases, your manufacturer may therefore have a factory at the other end of the world.

Amazon assumes no responsibility for the import of your products and does not act as an official importer. We'll talk a little bit about regulating imports to the US and the European Union, but you need to think about what that means to you. If you live in the US or in the European Union, you can import products and pay all customs fees. If you live elsewhere but want to sell in those areas, you need an agent.

This agent can act as an importer on your behalf, comply with all legal requirements, pay the applicable fees, and assist you in shipping these products to Amazon distribution centers. It goes without saying that an intermediary charges fees. You must also take this into account to evaluate your profitability.

Before you decide on a price, let's look at which Amazon invoices and which services are included in these charges.

The last change to Amazon's FBA tax was in early November. Since many of their warehouses are running at full capacity, they recommend that sellers send only items that they believe should be sold by the end of 2016. That does not mean that all other products are busy being rejected - it's just a matter of shipping inventory. For the next year higher fees may apply at this time.

Monthly storage fees increased by more than $ 1.15 per cubic foot of occupied space. However, Amazon has also lowered the rate per weight to offset this increase in storage fees.

If you are already an Amazon reseller, you can calculate the FBA conversion fee based on your product codes. If you are fresh to selling on Amazon, you can use this US and UK calculator to estimate the amount of commissions and fees you pay to Amazon.

A commission is the portion of the margin of the product that you pay to Amazon to improve your visibility. The fees are what you pay for storage, shipping and delivery.

If you've tried to calculate the fees for some of your products, you've probably found that higher-margin products are better for selling through FBA.

With regular cost reviews in mind, you might want to run a very dynamic line of products: Be prepared to remove all products that seem to be stored in the Amazon warehouse without being sold. An idiot-proof repayment agreement with your manufacturer can be helpful here. Product categories such as clothing and toys generally have very high margins.

Then there is the question of competition with other sellers. In most cases, different sellers rate the same product differently. As an FBA seller, you should NEVER set an unaffordable price for your product, even if you can get away with a price slightly higher than a third-party. It is useful to consult the prices of competitors and to agree with the price of the highest-rated seller.

When pricing a product for FBA, the following points should be noted:

A. If in doubt, always use a price calculator.

B. The fees are the fees that Amazon charges you for some of the work. A commission is what it costs to give you a sales window. Although commission is charged on the products sold, fees will be charged for the products of the Amazon warehouse. Amazon frequently revises its fees, albeit slightly.

C. Ideally, higher-margin products are better to sell through the FBA. If you are competing with other sellers, adjust the price of the best-rated seller or Amazon, depending on the competition.

AMAZON RULES AND REGULATIONS

Of course, you must follow certain rules if you want to sell by this method. We have divided them to reflect the rules in the United States and the United Kingdom. Some of them may overlap.

FBA rules in the United States

If you ship from another country to an American Amazon warehouse, you must be the official importer (IOR) of the shipment. An IOR ensures that the products comply with local laws and that the appropriate number must be provided to Amazon so that they can list your products.

If you return the products from the warehouse to your manufacturer, Amazon will not ship internationally. You must provide a return address, retrieve the shipment, and return it to the manufacturer.

The choice of the distribution center depends exclusively on Amazon. Some products that can not be part of FBA may still be sold by you as a third party vendor.

FBA rules in the UK

If you are not present in the United Kingdom and would like to sell products from another country via Amazon UK, you must hire someone to handle the shipment until it is released.

As in the US, Amazon determines which distribution center your products should be sent to. Responsibility for damaged products that are transported to a distribution center rests with your carrier. If you mislabel your product, it will be renamed by Amazon for an additional fee or returned to you.

You can terminate the FBA program at any time and there is no minimum vesting period.

Risk Mitigation when selling through FBA

Very few FBA sellers said they were dissatisfied with Amazon's service. Although Amazon does not guarantee the delivery time, anyone who has already been a customer will know that delivery is normally in the specified window. However, as a retailer, making wrong decisions can cost you money, especially because of the cost.

Here are some risks that you can best minimize.

Do not go all burning weapons. Choosing fifty products from international manufacturers and listing them all can work, but it certainly costs you a bomb. Also, consider the cost of return to the manufacturer if the products are not sold. Instead, start with a small selection of products and a decent stock.

If possible, choose product categories with a higher profit margin. In this way, you can compensate for the fees and commissions of Amazon.

Avoid price wars. If a product has a good sales ranking, it means the product has recently been sold. This is an indicator, but no guarantee that the same product will be sold again.

Apart from these aspects, things can and do go wrong with stocks as big as Amazon. Some mix cases have been reported where you are credited (or Brickbat) for a similar product owned by another seller. To reduce delivery times, Amazon may ship the products from the nearest warehouse, even if the order is yours and the product is yours.

Tracking Your FBA Orders

Since the product you own is yours, even if Amazon is responsible for the delivery and processing, you are the recipient of the notifications. This is the price you pay to use a warehouse that you have no control over. Billing and billing products sold through FBA may seem complicated, but it can also be quite simple:

The fees of Amazon are very different. For example, suppose someone orders a unit of your product and Amazon charges $ 5. If you had to order two items, Amazon's fees do not add up to $ 10 but are generally lower. For accounting reasons, this can be impractical because you would need to price the product separately for each product unit. In such cases, creating your billing worksheet with Amazon as a customer can help you.

With some retail software, you can track invoices for all FBA orders and quickly integrate them into the accounting software of your choice.

If Amazon is the term partner, how can you track returns and exchanges?

In most cases, no substitution is required for the replacement. The returned product will be added to

Amazon's inventory and a replacement product will be delivered. You can track these changes on your FBA inventory page.

For products that have been returned, Amazon uses a double approach:

When the product is once again in a salable condition, Amazon will re-add it to your inventory. The amount of the refund of your collections will be deducted and returned to the customer.

If the product is not in the sell status, Amazon determines who is responsible for you, the seller, or Amazon. If the damage occurred while processing, Amazon will not charge your collections. If the damage is yours, Amazon will charge you the reimbursement amount of your current collections. In both cases, the product will not be included in your already existing inventory.

Amazon usually has a 30-day window for returning products. Sometimes he can make exceptions to his right of return. In this case, you will not pay the reimbursement amount out of your own wallet.

Although most personal hygiene items can not be returned, they will not be added to your inventory as soon as they are accepted.

Sales in other markets via the FBA

With Amazon, you can execute orders received on other channels through the distribution centers. The most obvious benefit is that your inventory and inventory are not limited to Amazon. You can only use Amazon as a fulfillment center and process your orders through other channels. Amazon does not charge a commission for such orders, but you must pay fees: order management, picking and packing, and weight management fees are always charged by Amazon. The full fee schedule for the USA can be found here.

If you use Amazon for multi-channel sales, your shipping costs are significantly lower than when you try to process an order yourself. Besides, they can arrive even faster. Most buyers are willing to pay for this added value, and you get a higher profit, even if you set the price of your product at the price of a competitor.

An important detail to keep in mind is that FBA is currently processing orders on other channels only when shipped domestically. So, if you have many international buyers for these products, this option will not work.

With FBA, you can focus on three things in contrast to traditional online commerce: finding the right products, listing them on Amazon, and selling them. Everything else is done by someone else.

By closely monitoring your product inventory and sales ranking for a combination of products, you can compare the sales of your products with other successful products. That way, you can customize your product line.

As with any retail store, you will need to find the right manufacturers you can trust and who can deliver products at competitive prices. If you find a reliable set of people, never release them.

Do not forget to advertise. Ask people in your social circles to buy products from you. Advertise your offers. Talk to your family and friends and ask them to tell their friends. So many business people fear that someone else could persecute and bankrupt them if they share their business idea. But if you do not tell people what you are doing, you are already losing sales potential. Even if one of them picks up your idea and tracks it to T, they are not you.

We would also like to denote that FBA is a great option for online beginners and retailers. However, this may not make up the perfect solution for brands seeking a unique presence in the marketplace.

If there is one area where many new Amazon FBA vendors are not outstanding, it must be Amazon Inventory Management.

Let's take a quick look at why properly managing your Amazon inventory is one of the keys to the success of your Amazon FBA business.

3 Reasons Why Proper Amazon Inventory Management Is Vital

Amazon sellers probably hate losing almost as much money as they like. And while Amazon's inventory management does not seem to be a big deal, it can ultimately cost you hundreds, if not thousands! - Dollars on Amazon.

With Amazon Inventory Management you can...

1 - prevent bearing failures.

If you are out of stock on Amazon, it can cost a lot of money for a variety of reasons. First, and most obviously, if your product is not available on Amazon, it will not be sold. Then Amazon kidnappers can steal your list and take advantage of your negligence - it even happened to us! And finally, when your ad is dead, your rank suffers. If Amazon is no longer in stock, you must press the reset button for your entire company! Avoid it at all costs!

2 - Avoid expensive storage costs in the long run.

On the other side of the Amazon inventory management spectrum, the stock is too large. In the past, Amazon was quite casual with its sellers about how much inventory they could keep in distribution centers. In less than a month, however, Amazon tackles slow and sluggish stocks. You're introducing new long-term storage fees, and if you're not ready, you can quickly lose hundreds (and thousands!) Of dollars in a single day.

3 - Increases the available space on your Amazon Fulfillment Center storage.

After all, you probably want to expand your business with Amazon, right? But did you know that Amazon restricts the inventory in its distribution centers? It's true If you're not using Amazon Best Practices, you may not be able to obtain new products from Amazon. This could really slow down your growth potential. So continue with your index performance score!

How can I properly manage Amazon inventory?

Pay attention to your measurements! Fortunately, Amazon Seller Central provides sellers with a scorecard that tells you how to apply your Amazon inventory management practices: the service inventory. This number is located in the Inventory Planning widget of Amazon Seller Central.

What is this tool -   Amazon Seller Central Inventory Planning Widget?

When you sign in to Amazon Seller Central and scroll down, your inventory planning widget is right under your "Sales Summary" and "Global List" (or "Most Fun") widgets. There is also a lot of vital information about this tool.

This widget contains the following:

Inventory Performance Index - The Amazon score for the quality of your Amazon inventory management (see details below).

Number of storage days: How old is your stock on average?

Stock replenishment today - what products are you currently?

Excess units - what products should you remove from distribution centers?

UGS with blocked inventory - Which products have unsaleable units in distribution centers?

Notifications - Amazon tips on managing your inventory.

What is your Amazon Inventory Performance Index Score?

Amazon's Inventory Performance Index Score (IPI) refers to the metric that Amazon uses to "judge" the quality of your inventory on Amazon. The IPI provides a number between 0 and 1000. Ultimately, your IPI performance determines the amount of Amazon allocated space.

How the Inventory Performance Index relates to your Amazon storage limits.

This is how the IPI works, as it was explained by Amazon.

Individual sales accounts have the same storage restriction, which does not level up or decline.

Professional seller accounts may not have such storage restrictions based on the following criteria:

- Vendors who have an inventory performance index of 350 or higher will have unlimited storage for standard-sized items, oversized clothing, and shoes.

- Suppliers whose inventory index is below 350 six weeks before the end of the quarter will be informed of their possible storage limits. If your score is still below 350 on the last day of the quarter, your next quarter limits will apply.

- Vendors who do not have an inventory performance index will receive default storage limits until enough data is collected to generate a rating.

How do I keep my inventory value above 350?

Amazon examines four key drivers that drive your IPI. The code to keeping your IPI above 350 are these factors. But what is that?

The 4 main factors that influence the inventory performance index:

Overstock - Do you have too many stocks in Amazon distribution centers?

Sales Rate: Does your stock sell well relative to the amount of stock you have in stock?

Stranded Inventory - Do you have unsaleable units in Amazon distribution centers?

Evaluate in stock - Are you often out of stock of popular products?

Controlling these factors strengthens your IPI. Simply log in to your vendor page to resolve potential issues related to these factors. Scroll to the Inventory Planning widget and click on your score. Your inventory performance page will open.

First of all, Amazon will show you how individual influencing factors affect each other. By scrolling down the screen, you can fix any outstanding issues related to your inventory.

What is an overstock?

The amount of excess units is the number of units for which the inventory cost is likely to be higher than the cost of an action (eg, price reduction to increase sales or eliminate excess units). This value is depending on product demand and costs (including fees, unit costs, and capital inflow costs).

How to Manage Excess Inventories

First, you can sell it. It probably seems easier said than done, right? Fortunately, Amazon equips you with some tools to steer you in the right direction. Amazon PPC lets you sell more inventory. Vouchers and giveaways can also be helpful, especially in combination with a free website like Jump Send. And do not forget that you only lower the total sale price!

The other method of managing excess inventory is to use Amazon's deletion services. In fact, there are three ways to erase stocks: removal, deletion of delivery address and liquidation.

What is the sales quota?

Your Amazon sales rate is a ratio of your sales divided by the average of your storage units. For example, if you had an average of 300 units in your inventory over the past 90 days and sold 250 units, your sell price would be $ 0.83. Amazon considers everything below 0 (low). To stay "in the green" you need a sales quota of at least 2.0.

How to improve your sales rate?

The methods for improving your sales quota are similar to those for managing excess units. First, try to increase your sales. However, if you feel you have reached a plateau and know what your monthly revenue will be, try keeping the Amazon FBA inventory at about half of your 90-day estimate. So, if you normally sell 200 units a month, you should never store more than 300 units on Amazon (600 units on sale / 300 on average = transfer rate of 2.0).

If you already have too much inventory on Amazon, delete it now. Of course there are costs associated with it. But some fees are now much better than if Amazon charges you high storage costs in the long run. Or even lose your ability to carry new products!

What is a failed inventory?

Locked inventory refers to FBA inventory in distribution centers that have no active offer associated with them and are therefore not offered for sale to Amazon customers. This often happens with damaged inventory being returned or simply lost in the limbo of the Amazon distribution center.

One important note: you can not send other units of a product to Amazon if the inventory is locked! If you have a locked inventory, you will not be able to send other blocked product units to an Amazon distribution center.

How do I manage blocked assets?

Amazon has four methods for managing locked inventory. The method for managing locked inventory depends on why it is initially locked.

Here are the four methods:

Edit the list filled in by Amazon. This occurs when your product is in a processing center, but for some reason is listed as a filled-by-merchant product.

Create a new list. This is the case if the product was sent to Amazon but does not have a list. You must create a list for this product.

Create a removal order. This is the case if the product is completely unrealizable (damaged or returned).

Relist. If you simply want to offer the product for sale because you or Amazon have it closed, all that is required is for you to click this button and it should reappear.

What is the FBA stock price?

The FBA Inventory Rate is the percentage of time that your FBA refill products were in inventory for 30 days, weighted by the number of units sold in the last 60 days. Basically, Amazon tells you that you need to stock popular products. As mentioned previously, out-of-stock issues can seriously damage your Amazon FBA product list. Therefore, it is essential to stay informed.

How you can improve your FBA equity ratio

Of course you have to stay in stock! Of course, when dealing with foreign suppliers, this is not the easiest thing in the world. In fact, I would say that this is probably the hardest case to master. Even the products of Jungle Scout are exhausted!

Here are some vital tips you should keep in mind:

- Always try to stock sales for at least three months. Of course, you will not be able to keep all of your shares in Amazon, not if you want to get a good sales quota. You need to keep some of your inventory in a distribution center. If you have less than three months of sales in stock, immediately place an order with your supplier. So, if you run out of inventory, your new inventory should arrive.

- Follow suggestions from Amazon when your stock runs low. However, Amazon stinks a bit to predict when orders should be placed. Amazon reports low inventory when my inventory exceeds the remaining 14 days. With shipping times and times of 45 to 60 days, there is therefore a shortage of storage.

- Use Forecastly Inventory Management Software to keep track of your inventory. Forecasts know your appointments, your delivery times and the exact amount of your inventory to make sure you do not run out. It's like a crystal ball for your business. And the best part? We offer a 14-day free trial! So, if you do not like it, you do not have to keep it.

HOW TO FIND AND SELL HOMEMADE PRODUCTS

If you want to build your own online business, it's no better than selling private label products with Amazon's Fulfilled by Amazon (FBA) program.

It's simple enough, and there are many tools to help you succeed. Here are nine (9) basic steps for success:

1. Think about product ideas.

Ideas can come from anywhere. Here are some interesting tips to find killer ideas for private label products.

- Every time I search or shop for a business, I look for new trendy products. These are usually newer things; things that Wal-Mart and Target have not yet saved.

- Amazon itself is a second place to look for product ideas.

Search the departments and subcategories for new products (be sure to check the Recent Messages columns!).

- Find out about other providers' offerings in the Amazon showcases and product lists.

- Consult the Web to find ideas for cool products.

Social media has always had an idea of a wild and virulent product. Also discover Kickstarter and IndieGoGo, where brilliant inventors find new and innovative ways to showcase their products.

2. Consider specific product attributes.

So, what type of trademarks should you try to sell? If you are just beginning I strongly advise that you start with products with the following features:

Small and light. Your product must be able to fit in a small flat box and weigh no more than a pound or two. Shipping by the manufacturer and then, if applicable (by you or by Amazon FBA).

Not seasonal. The sale of your product should NOT depend on the season. Examples of seasonal products: Christmas lights, Valentine's gifts, winter clothes, etc. Avoid them as much as possible.

Not regulated. Some products, such as food, toys and batteries, are accompanied by "papers" that can make the sale of this product more difficult. I recommend that you stick to things that are easy to make and spread. Articles that do not require a lot of legal paperwork and / or certifications.

Easy. It can be fun to sell electronic products, but they often cause headaches and customer service issues. The same goes for fashion and clothing. You may need to use multiple colors and sizes for the same SKU.

3. Carry out a market research.

Once you've found some interesting products that you want to sell as private label products, you need to do some market research to see if it's worth the sale.

These days, you can skip the hard way - with a spreadsheet and lots of time looking at product lists. There are now applications like Jungle Scout's Chrome Extension, which you can use to search for products immediately.

This is how it works:

1. Search Amazon.com with your product idea as a search term.

2. Once the search results page loads, click the "JS" button on the right side of your browser's search/address bar to open the Jungle Scout Chrome extension (you'll need to purchase and download the extension) for this to work).

3. Check the product data. Chrome Extension shows you average monthly sales, average product reviews, and more for search results.

And that's it!

Of course, you need to know what criteria to look for. Products that sell on average between 250 and 400 units per month are usually a good idea.

4. Suppliers and manufacturers of research products.

Now that you've got the idea for the ideal product and reviewed the sales data with the Jungle Scout Chrome Extension extension, all you have to do is buy something!

Now, we have Alibaba for this. If you are unfamiliar with Alibaba, Alibaba is more or less the Chinese Amazon country, so we can buy bulk and bulk products directly from foreign manufacturers. And Alibaba is not only easy to use, but also safe, as all suppliers are carefully controlled.

Here are the basic steps to finding potential suppliers for your private label product on Alibaba:

- Create a buyer account at Alibaba.com.

- Do a search for your product on Alibaba; The product database of Alibaba works similar to Amazon.

- Look for product lists that resemble the idea of a private label product that you want to sell.

- Send a message to the supplier/manufacturer of the product for more information about the product. Ask the following questions:

- What is the unit price for this product if I order 500 units (or how many units I want to order)?
- Can I send a sample home? If so, what are the costs?
- Which payment terms and methods do you accept?
- How can I customize this product?

It is usually best to contact 3 to 5 suppliers for one product. For each of these suppliers, order a sample of the product.

5. Finish your logo, design and packaging.

Being a private label product, you can put our own logo on the packaging and on the product itself. If you are unfamiliar with graphics, you can use professional, low-cost designers to create eye-catching logos for your products on independent websites like the Jungle Market.

In addition, you should differentiate the design of the product from other products that are already on the market. And you do not have to be an engineer to customize your products. Sometimes, personalization can be so simple that the color of the product is changed or the product management is extended a bit.

Finally, try to offer the best possible packaging. Reflective packaging enhances the customer experience. You can also add the URL of your brand's website, useful information and more on your packaging to improve your marketing efforts.

6. Determine your success strategy.

Of course, it is only half the battle to know what you sell and how to make private label products. You also need a way to bring your products to your customers. However, there are a variety of ways to respond to your orders.Some people fill their own goods from their garage or even their own warehouse. Others use third-party distribution centers to ship their goods.

You can also choose to rely on the internal execution service of Amazon: FBA. Since its launch in 2008, FBA has changed the game for Amazon sellers. Not only do you have access to Amazon 2.5 billion monthly shoppers, but Amazon also manages the items or products for you.

All you have to do is send your inventory to Amazon. From there, store, fetch, pack and ship your goods for you - not to mention the fact that they also manage your customer service.

7. Choose your manufacturer.

What is the next step after all your ducks are lined up? Thanks to your market research, you know what you will sell and how much it is likely to sell once it is registered with Amazon. In addition, you have created an attractive logo, design and packaging. And you know that Amazon will fulfill you completely.

Then it's time to pick a manufacturer. You can remember in step 4 that we recommend contacting 3-5 potential manufacturers for your private label product and ordering samples from each one. This part of the decision-making process is extremely important. You have to do things well.

And you can learn a lot about the manufacturer, depending on how fast he sends you samples, what the status of the pattern is upon arrival, and what communication is required to track its status. Most times, these factors are more important than the actual cost of the product.

One mistake you want to avoid is to contact the manufacturer with the lowest cost, even though the quality of the product and your communication with the supplier are less than excellent. Of course, you want your costs to be low, but sometimes the cheapest product is not always the best product.

Instead, it is better to use the lowest prices to negotiate lower prices with manufacturers who have better communication and order-fulfillment capabilities.

Once we have selected our supplier, we will arrange for payment according to our preferred method as most vendors accept Alibaba's PayPal or Trade Assurance to securely process payments.

It takes about 3-4 weeks for a manufacturer to create a product, and then 1-2 weeks to send it to the nearest Amazon sales representative or the nearest Amazon distribution center. This 4 to 6 week period is the perfect time to create your Amazon list.

When creating an Amazon list, first ensure that everything is ready for publication and launch in advance. Second, great product photos are a must. It is better that you contact a specialist unless you have serious photography knowledge. If you're having trouble finding a photographer, the internet is a great place to find quality freelancers.

8. Then the title.

This is one of the most relevant elements of your Amazon Private Label product list. That way, Amazon can determine where your product should appear in its database.

Make sure that the keywords you refer in your title are important, otherwise your product will end up in the wrong category and will not be seen by your potential buyers.

For example, if you sell "Plastic Bottles" and want to classify this keyword, you must put "Plastic Bottles" at the beginning of the title. Then follow this group of keywords with secondary and tertiary keywords that you also want to rate. Finally, add the most powerful features and benefits of your products to the product description field and the chips.

These help customers make a purchase decision when they click on your page. The more your private label item or product meets their needs and desires, the more likely they are to buy.

9. Optimize your list to increase sales.

While much of the Amazon FBA brand sales process aims to "set and forget," you still want to make sure that your product list does everything in its power to increase sales. Amazon's personal advertising system - Amazon PPC - is an excellent way to draw attention to your private label product.

At Amazon PPC, bid on "sponsored ads". These ads help your product turn up on the first page of search results, remarketing ads outside of Amazon, and even on the product pages of your competitors. You can report on Amazon Seller Central to find out which keywords are being sold/converted. That way, you can determine which keywords you want to bid over PPC for.

In addition, you can use a Keywords Search Tool to find out which keywords your competitors use to make sales. After a couple of weeks of correcting and tweaking your bids, you can double or even triple them! - Your sales on Amazon.

Once you're familiar with Amazon PPC and the Amazon sales process, you can use other tools to test the effectiveness of the various items in your Amazon FBA branded product list.

A / B tests (or split tests) are an effective way to determine what works and what does not. When you run split tests, you run two concurrent tests that make minor changes to your list of products (for example, master image, price, and so on).

Then automated software like Splitly will help you see what works and what does not. You will sometimes be surprised to learn that the pictures and titles that you believe have caused sales are what has hurt you.

Pricing for private label products on Amazon.

One question that is often required is how to effectively evaluate Amazon products. Most new sellers instinctively set a very low (or even lowest) price for their product, but that's a big mistake. You should rarely set the price of my private label product so that it costs less than my competitors. Instead, try to bring out my product in a different way. Whether it's about better design and packaging, a stricter sales and marketing language in the product list itself or even great customer service, you should generally try to keep your price level below 20% of the average selling price of your competitors.

For example, if you find that "measuring cups" sell to Amazon for about $ 25.00, try to sell for no less than $20 or more than $30. In addition, you should always try to launch private label products on Amazon that cost between $ 20 and $ 50. If you earn less than $ 20, it can be hard to make a profit after deducting product costs and advertising costs. On the other hand, if you exceed $50, you get slower conversion rates and poor results of value-based valuation.

Examples of Private label products on Amazon

- Daily Planners
- Hats
- Measuring cups

Make sure you do some personal research as the market can (and will) change at any time. Perhaps the most important advice that can give to any new salesperson starting out on Amazon is simply to trust the process and allow yourself to grow.

Five years (or so) later, the nine success stories listed above will continue on the path to success, whether Amazon's terms of use change or market trends change.

As previously said, wrong prices, incorrect ratings, or poor customer service can bring your Amazon adventure to a halt faster than you think. For many, it makes Amazon difficult, but your pricing strategy on Amazon must be extremely simple and customer-focused. Your goal is to create as much revenue as possible, get real product reviews, and provide the best customer service to your Amazon customers.

3 steps to successfully sell at Amazon

Before you start, always think about your ultimate goal: You want your products to appear in the first three positions of the first page of search results for your most relevant keywords. In addition, you want to create on Amazon a long-term brand, with which Amazon can promote your products on the detail page of your product.

Here are the three (3) steps to successfully sell at Amazon:

1. Optimize the detail page of your product.

Before you think about increasing traffic, setting up a marketing budget, or refining your Amazon pricing strategy, you need to familiarize yourself with the basics. For Amazon, this means you'll need to tweak the details page of your Amazon product for Amazon's organic search results. The vast majority of Amazon sales are through search, with over 70% on the first page of Amazon search results. It is advised to spend a lot of your time optimizing your Amazon search products.

2. Create your prices for Page One on Amazon.

If you make a misstep, you may lose money or sell nothing. Determining the right price on Amazon does not have to be so difficult for branded products that you have no competition on your Amazon product page. In general, you must consider two variables for each product sold on Amazon because you want to achieve the following:

A. You want to make profit (find the lowest price)

B. You want to maximize the profit (find your highest possible price)

Now, here are the variables you must consider:

➢ You have to consider all your costs and the price you have to pay to be profitable with those costs on Amazon. You have to calculate your minimum price.

Your price must be competitive with your keywords in order for your product to appear on the first page of Amazon search results. More than 70% of Amazon sales are generated on the first page of organic search. Nobody will find and order your overpriced product on page 23.

How to calculate your Amazon minimum price:

In order to work effectively on Amazon, you must know all your costs, take them into account and then determine your minimum price. Below is a list of the costs that you need to consider in your equation:

- Acquisition cost
- Delivery
- Inch

- Payment cabling
- Amazon Commission
- Amazon FBA fee
- Customers return fee

For all returns, Amazon will retain 20% of the original commission as the return cost.

- Your own return costs (costs for return, disposal and product deduction)
- Variable overheads

You also have to consider some costs per category. For example, if you sell clothes, Amazon will commission a BAF shipping fee.

How to find your floor price:

Forget the inflated prices of your product! Amazon will tell you your price for the upper floor. Always remember that your ultimate goal is to place your products on the first page of Amazon search results. This is where the magic works and you can really sell volume.

➢ Consider the competition around you

However, it's one thing to put your products on the front page with important marketing resources (such as extensive introductory discounts, giveaways, or a large Amazon-sponsored product budget) that will keep your product on the front page and generate sustainable and profitable organic revenue. To keep your products on the first page, you need to consider the competition around you.

It's easy to rate. Just search for the top three keywords for your product and see the prices for the search results on the first page. Then answer this question: Are your prices within a reasonable range of the prices you find there?

In our experience, you can earn 20% more than the highest price listed on the first page of search results. For example, if the highest price you find on the first page is $ 40, our top floor price should be $ 48. If your price is higher, you'll probably never reach the top of Amazon search results.

3. Keep your prices constant with exceptions.

Keep your prices stable to win customer trust and build a long-term sustainable brand on Amazon. There are of course exceptions. The main reason for price differences is the increase in your sales rank, which will later increase organic sales.

The second reason for price decreases is the cross-selling of your products, which also translates into a higher sales ranking for all products included in the cross-sell promotion. Typically, this means lowering your prices to a break-even point or below profitability. This happens most often when introducing new products.

Your company may deviate from our standard prices mainly in the following contexts:

A. New products launched - You may offer all customers an introductory discount of 15% - 50%

B. Cross-selling

C. Stock clearance - If you have excess supplies, this can help you get rid of them. It can also revive a dead product. Before you ever think about lowering prices below profitability, always remember that you can only have fun (ie, succeed) once you can sell Amazon on Amazon organic sales with an appropriate profit margin.

How to direct traffic to your Amazon products

Without traffic, there is no sale. It is not enough to list your product on Amazon and hope that traffic and sales will be successful. Today, not only do you need Amazon organic traffic, but you also need traffic from external sources on your Amazon product page. There are many stories of people who had a lot of buzz around their products but little sales. The excitement failed to translate into any tangible sales. Here are the top three proven strategies that you can use today to generate most of our traffic on our Amazon product pages:

1. Create an e-mail list.

A mailing list is a marvelous way to increase your product launch revenue. We use our mailing list to send our customers directly to our new Amazon product pages. We also give them a free discount code for buying products and often see a good start to the sale. As an Amazon salesperson, you might be wondering how to create a list because you can not get the actual email addresses from customers and you should not write them for marketing purposes.

Start with these three simple methods to create your own list:

- Add a registration field to your website. For example, a newsletter subscription, an e-book download and much more.

- Communicate your newsletter subscription option on your social media channels and packaging.

- After your sale to Amazon you can send an e-mail to your customer. Show them this email on your newsletter subscription page. A good tool of choice is ConvertKit, which has a very user-friendly interface and allows you to easily identify your customers and create custom newsletter campaigns.

2. Place targeted Facebook ads.

In 2014, many organizations transferred a large portion of their budget to external ads from Google on Facebook. Today, Facebook ads are a major source of paid external traffic. On Facebook, you have many advertising options and do not need an existing fan base. The benefit of Facebook ads is that you can define your audience and create a message that appears directly in a user's Facebook feed.

For example, for a new product, you may create a target group of females between the ages of 20 and 30 or men under the age of 40 with an interest in reading.

With these ads, you will experience impressive results.

One problem with these ads however is you may not be able to tell immediately if they are were profitable. Today, it is no longer conceivable for you to do business without analysis - spend quality time developing analytics for quantified markets! Working with analytics, you will see your Amazon marketing performance catapulted into new dimensions on Facebook. With the analysis you finally know if:

- Your advertising on Facebook is worthwhile. They are really aimed at the target groups who buy their products on Amazon

- Your ad generates revenue

3. Use Amazon sponsored product locations.

Amazon sponsored products are by far the fastest way to get your product on the first page of Amazon search results. Amazon-sponsored products work just like Google AdWords, which offers search terms. When someone looks for your product on Amazon, you can buy an ad based on those keywords and your offer will appear next to the best results.

The big advantage of Amazon sponsored products is that the installation is very easy. You can do it in a couple of minutes. However, you will need to carefully and regularly manage your account, even in a simple interface, to avoid an explosion in the marketing budget.

There are two main reasons for this.

First, Amazon constantly improves the algorithm, which means that your successful campaign loses money this morning.

Second, as more sellers enter the market, competition for your ads becomes increasingly difficult. Amazon has also started the Sponsored Products program for Amazon Retail customers. A better idea is to use an internal person who closely monitors your campaigns.

4. Refer to all product links to Amazon.

You may think: "Why should I send my customers to Amazon if I already have my own website?" The main reason is that your ultimate goal is to be on the first page of the research and, if possible, to be among the top three. This is where the large money is made, not by a single sale on your website. In addition to our website, every link from Facebook, Twitter, YouTube, Instagram, our blog, and our e-newsletter will take you to a specific Amazon product page.

You can build a high ranking in the search engines of your own online shop through content marketing and contact with influencers to get backlinks to relevant and high-quality websites.

5. Put your products in the hands of bloggers and YouTubers.

Youtube is the second largest search engine in the world. It is really nice to have a lot of reviews on your products so that you are the first on a search, no matter where you are looking for them. Remember, Google has Youtube. Choose YouTubers and Bloggers that best fit your product and brand and offer free samples.

Here are some tips for raising awareness:

- Make sure you talk about your campaign and solve a problem for your audience. Do you know that they regularly receive tons of these e-mails?
- Keep a summary list of your contacts and those who respond. Use this to create your own list of influence.
- When you submit your products for the exam, give them only your best-selling product. Put all your eggs in a basket. Keep in mind that this product should be among the top three on the first page of search results. You must therefore ensure that all traffic to this product is routed.

6. Maximize the packaging of your product.

Make the most use of your packaging. You can include in your packaging, discount codes, business cards or small booklets that customers can use with their next order or give to their friends. This way, you have a free easy way of marketing to your customers. Customers will speak to their friends about you and buy more boxes for themselves.

You can also use your best customer voices and testimonies to build trust. Make your best offer on the outer packaging of your key products and add a customer case study or testimonial in a small booklet.

7. Create effective Google campaigns.

Facebook ads and Amazon-sponsored products have fundamentally changed the game of advertising. Today you need to use Google AdWords that can engage your target market and audience.

Concentrate on the brand name:

Focus on your brand name and the most specific keywords of your brand and product. You can derive a lot of Google traffic from users looking for your brand name.

Long-tail keywords in focus: In the long-tail sector, you should only create very specific campaigns for your products, which must include the product name, material, and color. For example, the words that are keywords of your product, phrases like "Black leather purse".

8. Get real product reviews

Without product reviews, you will not sell anything on Amazon. The number and quality of reviews are the most important aspects of your reviews to increase your conversion rate. Unfortunately, only 1 out of every 100 customers has submitted a review.

Here are some ways to increase the number of reviews of original products:

NOTE

Before we go into detail, a quick warning is needed as Amazon is currently attacking sellers buying fake reviews. Never joke with Amazon's policies.

- Avoid critical clubs and excessive gifts that do not comply with Amazon's Terms of Service.

- Do not give away a free product in exchange for an Amazon review.

Your goal should be to engineer trust with your customers and build a long-term brand on Amazon. Even if the customer sends out a warning that he has received the product for free, it will damage your product and there is a possibility that Amazon will remove all of these ratings or even block you.

You should do these instead.

1. Send an e-mail to your customers after purchase and ask for their opinion. You can use hacks like Feedback Genius to automate these steps.

Send the e-mail a few days after purchase. Ask neutrally and do not force them to drop a good review. Present a direct link to the review page, as many of your customers have probably never written a review. You can also take this opportunity to ensure that the product has been delivered properly and give the customer the opportunity to talk about their (good or bad) experiences to get the most out of the interaction and build a lifetime brand loyalty.

2. Use the supplier's "bad" reactions to get product ratings.

Customers often confuse the seller's comments with product reviews. Unfortunately, very good product reviews are often not very visible to other customers. Periodically review your suppliers' comments to see if people give positive feedback on the products and send them an email to write a product review.

3. Pay attention to the comments.

Everything on the Amazon product page is free to the public. In particular, the critical sections and comments are read by almost all future customers. This is your chance to get noticed. Comment on negative product reviews or reviews where a customer has a question. It's your chance to create a climate of trust and increase your conversion.

In addition, many customers who originally rated your product as negative may even replace it with a positive rating because they are grateful for your interest in their issue.

4. Ask customers who send you comments via email.

The simplest way to get product reviews on Amazon is to ask customers who tell you how much they like your product. If you receive an e-mail, a customer service call, or positive feedback about your social media channels, just politely ask them if they're ready to share their experiences with other Amazon customers.

HOW TO PROVIDE EXCEPTIONAL CUSTOMER SERVICE

You can not go wrong if your Amazon customer benefits from it. Amazon itself is the most customer-oriented company in the world. They expect the same standard from their sellers. Your best marketing tool on Amazon today is an exceptional customer service.

Your goal should be to develop a "wow" experience that helps spread word of mouth. To explain what a "wow" experience is, I mean one where the customer is happy, satisfied and genuinely in love with your product and brand. It is one in which you not only exceed expectations, but also exceed everything the customer could ask for or imagine! It is also one in which the customer is willing to recommend you to friends and colleagues. By aiming to give customers a "wow" experience, you can easily turn a negative output into a positive one.

Here are a few tips on providing exceptional customer service:

1. Startup your customer service on your Amazon product page.

All your customers start their customer journey on the product page. They read reviews, ask questions, read the comments of their provider and finally click the "Add to Cart" button. It is only fair then that you also begin your customer service journey on this page.

Set up a daily routine for your product pages that includes the following actions:

- Comment on negative product reviews and offer immediate help

- Answer the questions in the Questions and Answers section

- Actively manage the comments of your salespeople

2. Respond quickly to your customers and be generous.

The second pillar of your customer service is e-mail. You need to answer all emails within 24 hours or faster and strive to solve any customer service problem in a single communication.

Here are four ideas you can use to achieve this:

- Answer all emails within 24 hours

- Always include a solution in your first answer

- Simplify things for your customers

- Be generous

3. Be responsive on your social media channels.

Your customers will talk to you or with you and expect you to communicate with them on their favorite social media channel. Facebook and Twitter are best to use as your first customer service channels. You can exceed expectations and astonish your customers by answering all questions in less than an hour.

You should also set up a FAQ section on your website to answer frequently asked questions. Finally, send an easy-to-use contact form on your website.

One final note about your Amazon strategy: This whole process works the same way around the world and the potential is huge. Over 300 million active customers are waiting for you. With Fulfillment by Amazon, selling your products worldwide has never been easier.

USING FACEBOOK ADS FOR AMAZON MARKETING

If you are savvy with and are experienced with social media, you probably know the power of Facebook ads. Facebook has a virtually unlimited reach and knows more details about your friends than you. For Amazon sellers, this is a potential goldmine they can count on to increase conversions.

Creating an ad on Facebook is easy, and setting up your first ad takes just minutes. However, most people forget that creating advertising is a skill that requires special attention. It's not easy to find the right audience and start the race.

Here are three tips to help you place Facebook ads for your Amazon FBA company:

1. Create emotional copies

Facebook ads are what review class reviews call disruption marketing. Compared to Amazon PPC, where customers are actively looking for a product, Facebook users are less interested in buying. You have to break through to them and try to get their attention. You need to have your product examined so they can buy it. The most reliable way to get their attention is to make copies based on their emotions. How do you do it?

- Take advantage of the fear of missing persons or the FOMO mentality: People are afraid to be the last person they know. They tend to go into the crowd because they are afraid of missing out on something. Work with this mindset when writing your copies.

- Excite them: It is not impossible to excite people when they read on a phone screen. Gather the words you use and your tone. Use exclamation marks or uppercase letters. People who are upset get carried away and click on your ad.

- Invite immediacy: The best way to invite urgency is to offer something for a limited time. For example, you can offer a reduced price for the next few days. Just make sure your offer is strong enough to trick customers into buying.

2. Use high-quality pictures

The image of your Facebook ad is very similar to the image of your Amazon ad. Its main purpose is to grab enough attention for people to buy it. Some marketers use different images and test those that work best. Here are some keys to get the best image for your ad:

- Use images that imply trust: If possible, post a picture of a celebrity, influencer, or local person promoting your product. When people see someone famous uses the product they sell, it creates your trust.

- Tell a story: use carousel displays to tell a story with pictures. A good story is to show you how your product is changing your life for the better.

- Show them how it is used: If it's a product that needs to be assembled, show them how to assemble it using pictures. Create examples of how your product can be used in a real context for people to identify with.

- Always be up to date: Above all, consider optimizing your ads on Facebook to give them the same look, including your pictures. This increases brand awareness and the next time a person sees your ad, they automatically know what to expect.

3. Track sales, not clicks

A Facebook ad for a light bike with lots of flavor and parts does not automatically mean that it's profitable. It is easy to be immersed in all the clicks, comments, and sharing that you see, but it is not relevant if you do not turn them into paying customers. Marketers call these things metrics of vanity and that's all they are - vanity.

If you focus on those vanity metrics, you're likely to lose money instead of generating it. For example, if you advertise a light bike that costs $ 15, spend $ 10 on ads for each sale. It is not a good number. You only earn $ 5 per transaction, with no other expenses such as overheads. Even if the ads contain a hundred likes and comments, you lose money at a low conversion rate.

Focus first on the sale, then on the profitability measures. Follow every ad you start and calculate the amount of your income after deducting the cost. If you do it right first, you save a lot of money on advertising.

The tips above are the foundation for creating Facebook ads. Always write copies that evoke emotions, associate them with the right image and follow your standards in a religious way. Facebook users are usually not available to buy products, but may be willing to see your offers. As a merchant and business owner, it is your responsibility to stop them and pay attention to what you offer.

TO NOTE

In today's e-commerce world, Amazon is a real monster. We all know it and we use it all ... whether we want to say it or not. But today's consumers are not just using Amazon to buy products. They also use it to clarify prices (90% of consumers use Amazon to check the price of a product) to discover new products (72% of consumers visit Amazon to find product ideas) and look for new products search. Products (56% of consumers visit Amazon in front of all other websites).

Did you use Amazon for any of these purposes? I know that I have.

Here are other fascinating statistics from Amazon:

Amazon sells more than 12 million products, excluding books, wine, media and services. Amazon has more than 310 million active users, including 90 million Prime members in the US. Amazon Prime members spend nearly $ 1,500 a year. 7% of premium members buy something every day.

In 25 years, Amazon has grown exponentially. He sees more than 2,000 new salespeople every day. Whether you're a seasoned Amazon salesman or want to become one, this place can be intimidating.

That is why we have developed this guide to assist you to build a profitable marketing strategy and succeed in the Amazon jungle. Literally.

With about 12 million products and more, it is a dense jungle. It may seem almost impossible to succeed as a seller on Amazon, but the answer is actually quite simple: you have to think like a buyer.

Before you create an Amazon marketing strategy, you need to make sure that the pages in your Amazon product are ready for new buyers. You can do this by maximizing your pages to draw in buyers. (These practices also assist or support Amazon SEO - which we'll discuss later.)

Amazon is a remarkable platform because users visiting Amazon are already in a buying situation, unlike Google and other search engines. All traffic to your Amazon product pages can already be purchased, even if only prices are checked or new products are found.

As a salesperson, your job is to notice this audience and optimize your site to attract a potential buyer. Let us evaluate the specific components of your product pages, which are arranged from top to bottom. (If you are curious about what Amazon has to say, read the style guide for a quick start.)

1. **Product Title**

The title of your product is the first consumer launch of your product when browsing Amazon. Although your titles are concise, Amazon allows up to 200 characters. However, use this character limit wisely.

We recommend the following:

- Your brand name
- The name of the product
- Specific properties (such as size, color, material, quantity, etc.)
- One or two advantages or special values
- There are also some formatting rules for Amazon titles:
- Capitalization of the first letter of every word (except for words like "and").
- Use "and" instead of "&" and numbers ("10") instead of "ten" numbers.
- Do not place prizes, vendor information, promotions, and opinion-based text (such as "best" or "leader") in the title.

- Leave out details such as color or size if it is not the product.

Your title is the property of your choice for two things: product information and keywords. Most products are identical products. However, some sellers add a few more keywords to increase the likelihood that they will appear on Amazon's SERPs. In the end, your title should match the words buyers use to discover your product and inform them about your product before it gets to your page.

Tip: Use tools such as Merchant Words and Simple Keyword Inspector to search for potential keywords and their search volume.

2. **Product Images**

As your titles share information about your product, consumers use your images to decide if they want to investigate your merchandise page. On a long list of possible Amazon search results, merchandise images can highlight your product.

However, once a buyer has visited your product page, imaging is even more important: it can decide whether a consumer makes a purchase or not. Amazon allows up to nine product images. We recommend using them all only if you have nine relevant high-quality images. Amazon requires the image of your main product to be white and simple. Here are some key tips for your other eight product images:

- Capture your product from different angles.
- Show your product being used or tried by a real person (not a mannequin or a computer-created person).
- Include content put together by real customers - and write them on the image.
- Download images that contain charts, lists, or comparison charts of competitors. Amazon also offers buyers the opportunity to enlarge any image. For this reason, images of your products must be at least 1,000 x 1,000 pixels in size.

Tip: Test your stock images to see which most buyers convert (for example, an A / B test). Save your sessions, sales, conversion rates, and revenue over a period of a week or a month - and note which image was designated as the primary image. Then edit the image and capture the same data.

3. Important product features (bullet points)

The consumer exceeds the title of your product, the images, the price, and the purchase options (if any), he or she will find the key features of your product or chips. With these chips, you can deepen the features, benefits, features, and details of your product. Successful Amazon sellers use these chips to further develop their functions and benefits, and to resolve common questions, misunderstandings, or problems.

We recommend that you approach the list of key features of your product as follows:

- Write a paragraph for each bullet and contain two to four sentences or sentences that are relevant to the subject of this bullet.
- Write the first words of each chip in capital letters to highlight the function, benefit, or question that appeals to you.
- Treat these paragraphs as an advertising or marketing campaign. These paragraphs could be the key to converting visitors to the page.
- Do not waste space with obvious information from product images or the title of your product.

Tip: Read reviews, complaints, and frequently asked questions to find out what your customers love about your products and what they do not like. Add these points to your list and proactively record them.

4. Product description

If a consumer is going to describe your product, you can assume that he is about to make a purchase. How do we know that? Consumers need to scroll a bit to find it.

Seriously. You need to scroll through Amazon ads, sponsored products, and other information. When they come to describe your product, they expect you to learn more about your product and complete the purchase (or leave your site).

So use your product description to develop your product points, process a few lesser-known features and benefits, and possibly include some additional images of your product. Also, consider list details that distinguish your product from those of your competitors. In this section, Amazon provides basic HTML tags (bold, italics, and page breaks). Use them to avoid publishing a boring big paragraph.

Tip: Use Amazon's Enhanced Branded Content option to make your content more readable, professional, and consistent with your overall branding. We discuss how this is done next.

<u>Amazon Enhanced Brand Content</u>

With Enhanced Brand Content (EBC), you can update your Amazon product descriptions at no additional cost. Previously, Amazon had reserved EBC for products sold through Amazon and the vendor program as part of the vendor program. However, this feature has recently been made available to all sellers through Seller Central under Advertising.

EBC offers predefined templates that allow you to add additional features such as banners, spreadsheets, bullets, and interactive images and copies to your product description. If you simply open an Amazon seller account, you will not have access to EBC. You must also open an Amazon Seller Central account with a Pro subscription, register each of your trademarks with the Amazon Trademark Registry, and have a brand name for each brand name.

Amazon marketing strategy

Vendors need to develop an Amazon marketing strategy to lure consumers into their Amazon product pages and turn them into customers. Typically, an Amazon marketing strategy includes five components: Amazon Marketing Services, Amazon SEO, Feedback, Direct Marketing, and Affiliate Marketing.

After optimizing your Amazon product pages, you can drive traffic to your products with a thoughtful and cost-effective Amazon marketing strategy. Note: Most of these strategies work together (as you'll see). So you can always test one or two strategies simultaneously.

Amazon Advertising (or Amazon Marketing Services)

Amazon sellers market on the platform through Amazon Marketing Services (AMS). AMS is similar to Google ads because sellers only pay when buyers click on the ads. The service uses keywords, related products, and user interests to serve ads where users are most likely to click.

As a seller, you can choose how your product should be displayed. Product display ads appear on the side or bottom of Amazon SERPs and related product pages. When you click on it, product ads will appear on a product page. Sponsored product ads appear on the Amazon SERPs and product pages before the product description. Sponsored product ads always lead to a product page when clicked.

Search ads in titles are the most customizable Amazon ads. They appear at the top of Amazon's SERPs, and may include a personalized ad and a link to a branded landing page where you can offer personalized browsing, branding, and selected products. As with your Amazon marketing strategy, consider creating an Amazon ad strategy to better target your ads and drive business traffic to your product pages.

Amazon SEO

As I said earlier, Amazon is a very popular search engine. (To repeat the above, over 70% of shoppers visit Amazon to find new product ideas, and more than 50% are looking for products on Amazon.) Amazon is not just an electronic commerce website; It also functions as a search engine. And as a search engine, it will have its own optimization or SEO.

The Amazon search engine is called A9. It runs on its own algorithm and comes with unpredictable updates - similar to Google. The A9 looks different than Google: It only cares about its buyers (also called researchers) and its sellers. It's great if you shop ... but not so much fun selling.

However, it is important to consider this as a seller. Think like a shopper and you will be fine with A9. (Remember, we talked about tweaking your Amazon product pages to look like a buyer, which is one of the main reasons.) In terms of A9 and Amazon SEO, you want to optimize your content for three things: the ability to discover, relevance, and sell. In other words, you want buyers to see, click and buy your products.

Discoverability

First, let's talk about findability. Think: what helps shoppers find my products? Invest in Amazon advertising (as described above), as well as in Facebook and Google Ads, to increase traffic to your product pages.

Create product titles that are read naturally and reflect a handful of relevant keywords. Use special characters (for example, | or - or,) to make the title easier to read. Place the most relevant and searched terms first (in a meaningful order).

Take a look at the titles of the competitors, especially those who are among the first on the SERP. They do something good when they are considered high.

Use the background search terms from Amazon that are available under "Keywords" when you edit a product list. Amazon can contain up to 250 characters (spaces, commas, etc.). Use this space with care. Use words with a hyphen (as water-resistant) to cover all possible combinations as well as individual words.

Relevance

Then the relevance. Think: What helps shoppers to click on my products?

Make sure your product images are crystal clear and your product appears in the best light ... in the truest sense of the word. Buyers decide based on their main picture whether they click or not.

Although your product chips may not necessarily affect your product's ranking, they can add to the relevance of the product once a customer arrives at your site. Use relevant keywords in your bullets (especially those that you can not embed in your title) to encourage buyers to buy more keywords.

The same note applies to your product titles. Buyers will judge the relevance of the product.

Distribution

Finally sale. Think: what helps shoppers to buy my product? Make sure your product page meets the promise of the title and images of your product.

Optimize your product page for conversions. Present as many guest comments as possible - we have discussed this in earlier chapters.

5. Product reviews

Customer reviews and ratings are important. They are even more important in the world of e-commerce, where buyers can neither see nor touch a product before buying it. At Amazon, nearly 90% of buyers said they did not buy a product with less than three stars.

Amazon recognizes the power of user reviews and encourages customers to make their comments an integral part of each product page. Customers can view customer images, filter suggested keyword comments, search for content in reviews, sort ratings by stars, and view customer questions and answers.

As a seller, you must also give priority to announcements. You can make or break a buyer's buying decision - possibly more than your optimized product pages. Although you can no longer encourage reviews, you can ask your customers to complete them. Here are some options:

- Include a thank-you letter and a verification request for shipping your product

- Send a follow-up email with a verification request

- Sell a reviewable product

Finally, Amazon allows sellers to react to reviews. This is another way to build relationships with customers, express gratitude, and resolve issues or complaints.

Direct Marketing

Much of Amazon's marketing takes place within the platform (through advertising and SEO), but some vendors also follow traditional direct marketing methods. If they need extra work, they can be helpful in attracting loyal customers and possibly moving Amazon's activities to an e-commerce site (if you're interested).

Note: Carefully read Amazon's activities and actions for Prohibited Sellers to ensure you comply.

EMAIL

Have you ever ordered anything from Amazon and then received an email from the seller? It is always good for customers to receive emails thanking them for your purchase, requesting a product comment, and even offering a discount code for your next purchase.

It may be a surprise to the customer at first but they will understand your intent. Many vendors choose to implement separate e-mail marketing methods to promote their business and expand their list.

Tip: If you choose email marketing for your Amazon products, do not forget to ask subscribers if they want to join!

SOCIAL MEDIA

Some Amazon providers also create social media profiles for their brand. This is another way to communicate with current and potential consumers. Use your social media to distribute product updates, promote sales and gifts, and invest in paid advertising.

Tip: Share all your social media accounts on your Amazon brand page and product lists to build your followers list.

WEBSITE

Did you know that a lot more than 80% of Amazon sellers sell through other channels such as eBay, third-party websites and others? It's not uncommon to own and operate your own e-commerce website in addition to your Amazon store.

While Amazon can help you identify and subsidize your shipping and support costs, creating a separate website can help you strengthen your brand beyond Amazon and bring your own customers together. and subscribers.

Tip: If you do not desire to create and manage a complete website, first create a simple landing page. This will give your brand at least one online identity outside of your Amazon store and present another place to collect emails and promote your social media.

AFFILIATE MARKETING

It is so easy these days to scan a list of recommended products and, even better, send them directly to Amazon to find out which products interest you. Have you ever wondered how these products are on the list? Through affiliate marketing.

Affiliate marketing essentially involves the marketing of your products through a subsidiary - in this case Buzzfeed. In return for publishing/mentioning/ sharing your product, you pay a small fee when readers click and buy. It's a win-win situation that lets you generate sales, collect reviews, and educate your readers.

Tip: Access the Amazon Affiliate Program. It's free and easy to use and connects you instantly with approved partners.

Amazon does not seem so scary now, right? Yes, the platform can cover 12 million products, but as a seller, your priority must be given to your products only.

Also, note the following as you proceed:

First, maximize your product pages so that your marketing efforts can attract converted buyers. Then apply the Amazon Marketing Strategies mentioned above to generate more traffic and get more profits.

In two simple steps, your Amazon products will reach consumers wherever they are, whether they are looking for products, comparing prices, or buying. Between Amazon Retail and third-party suppliers, Amazon generated sales of approximately $ 120 billion last year in the United States. The majority of these sales were made by third parties. If you're a brand leader, the idea of placing your products on

Amazon is probably a bit scary. However, the reality is that your products are coming to Amazon, whether you want to be there or not, and that your competitors are already selling there.

Whether you sell or advertise on Amazon, you need to understand your relationship with this 800-pound gorilla so you can manage your brand, be competitive, and increase sales. Ignorance is not an option to deal with Amazon.

Let's take a minuter look at the challenges that Amazon has created for your business and see what processes you need to go through to succeed in an Amazon-dominated e-commerce world.

- Does your brand have an Amazon problem?

Let's define our concepts first. You can sell your products either to Amazon or Amazon. If you sell wholesale, Amazon offers to:

- Own the product.

- Meet price decisions.

- Decide what should be kept in stock.

You can also sell your products through third-party Amazon. It can get a bit complicated here.

Unauthorized seller on Amazon

Much attention has been paid to all unauthorized sellers on Amazon - companies that do not have a brand affiliate, but find ways to sell their products on Amazon. If you lose control of your inventory and other companies have access to your product, the Amazon Marketplace becomes a problematic channel.

You can not control the prices because you do not know who the sellers are. If you do not know them, how do you make sure the Amazon channel is focused on everything you do in all other channels you control?

Price transparency and lack of control: the worst-case scenario

Whether or not you manage your brand on Amazon, all of your retail partners can easily see what's happening in the marketplace. Many brands end up having embarrassing conversations with retailers saying:

"I can not afford these wholesale prices because they only cost 5% more on Amazon." to which the brand replies: "It's not our fault, we do not know who these companies are."

Unfortunately, it does not matter if you do not know who the third-party providers are. Consumers are not interested in who sells the products, and retailers only look at the results. The moral of the story is: If the consumer can still get the cheapest product on Amazon, your brand has a problem with the Amazon channel.

Control your brand on Amazon

By a brand sold on Amazon, what is implied is a company that has a registered trademark in the US. When dealing with unauthorized third-party vendors, many brands think:

"Perhaps if I complain long enough or loud enough about these sellers, I can scare customers away from them" But it is not always true.

Brands often use legal advice to send termination and cancellation messages, but rarely find this strategy convincing enough to get vendors to stop selling the product.

The gray market, the theory of first sale and your commercial rights

The reality is that there are many very sophisticated sellers on the gray market at Amazon and they are not scary. They are all legally represented and know how to sell their products on Amazon.

The doctrine of the first sale is a legal notion according to which every person in this country has the privilege to buy a product and then resell and resell it. These sophisticated sellers in the gray market know that they have legal protection through the doctrine of the first sale. You need to be more sophisticated as a brand if you want to protect your ability to control sales.

1. Get a mark to defeat the doctrine of the first sale

An important way to overcome the doctrine of first sale is to change the way you use a brand. You can structure your brand so that emphasis is not only placed on the name of your brand, but also the way the product is handled - how it is transferred from the retailer to the consumer.

There are approximately 75 different ways to define and apply a brand. If you can prove that a trademark problem exists, you can ask a court to decide in your favor and bypass the doctrine of the first sale as a legitimate way for an unauthorized seller to sell your products on the market.

If you take control of your brand, you can achieve the following:

- Do better in controlling the distribution without having to rely on sending these ugly letters to stop unauthorized sellers.

- Show that reselling your products without permission is actually a legal issue.

Resellers are selling their products illegally and can not hide behind the doctrine of the first sale. The management of a brand and the further monitoring of this brand often incur costs for the business activity. You must have the right kind of reseller policies online and use an anti-diversion language that says resellers and retailers are not allowed to sell the product to unauthorized third parties.

Lack of control is a motivational problem in retail.

However, the reality is simple: hardly any brand in the world has total control over sales. Brands are sold to retailers or dealers and their incentives may not match perfectly with the incentives of the chain.

As a brand, your aim is to sell many products and protect the value of the brand. The retailer or distributor, however, only cares about selling many products. These companies have no incentive to worry about the long-term value of your brand or whether you can get the high price you want based on the value of your brand. You therefore need to find a way to motivate your channel to do what you want and to sell your product at a higher price than a generic product.

Channel control is an economical saving

Although you probably cannot keep your channel clean all the time, for most of these highly developed gray market vendors, you can create enough obstacles to make them decide that it's too tedious to sell your brand. They will switch to another brand that will handle stamps very well. Your aim should be to keep your channel clean enough for you to pick up the Amazon Buy Box yourself, or at least to make sure your distributor has the buy box most of the time.

In the end, your pricing on Amazon will be stabilized and more in line with your pricing on all non-Amazon channels. And if your prices are consistent online and off-line, it's much easier to attract more retailers to sell your product.

There are numerous stories of organizations that have lost their distributors and their distributors had this to say:

There's no point in getting retailers to market your product because you have no control over what's happening at Amazon.

Once the brand gains control of what was happening on Amazon, it could bring back dealers who could then import their products into virtual circuits.

AMAZON ADVERTISING

We often think that Amazon is a place where products are sold, but it's also a place where businesses promote their products and get indexed on Google. It is always very useful to separate the sales part from the brand part.

If you are a brand that intends to stay in the market for a long time and understands that you will never 100% control your distribution, you have to keep in mind that Amazon is a gigantic website on which all listings are indexed.

Amazon ads are so indexed (usually number one or the number two in organic search results) that you're in a situation where your Amazon content will remain very visible even if it's not very good.

However, high visibility does not mean that you will sell more, especially if your content is mediocre. The trademark register is the right way to sell on Amazon, You will need to add your content to the Amazon catalog by registering it through a program called Brand Registry. This is an unpaid program that allows you, as a registered trademark in the United States, to ask Amazon to submit and block content directly.

Even if you do not sell any products on Amazon, you can at least block the content of all your trademark listings to reduce the risk that a new unauthorized salesperson associated with your product will sell a list of products if their content is inaccurate, incomplete or inconsistent.

Forget the fact that you do not want this unauthorized seller to be there. Accept the fact that this is likely to happen someday. Therefore, make sure the content on Amazon is of high quality and is consistent with everything you do in all other distribution channels.

Amazon FBA Business Tips: 12 common pitfalls that you should avoid as an Amazon FBA seller

When you start your Amazon FBA business, you are taking a risk. A wrong move can cost valuable time and money, if not worse. A mistake could trigger your business collapse before you start. The Amazon ecosystem can be confusing, but you can maximize your chances of success by providing a wealth of information.

So, if you're a new Amazon FBA seller, you're in luck. This is a list of the most viral mistakes you should avoid at the beginning of your FBA journey. Most of them focus on private label sales as more than half of Amazon FBA sellers offer one or more private label products.

The 12 Most Avoidable Amazon FBA Errors

1. Tracking the wrong resources

It's extremely easy, perhaps a bit too easy, to find courses, gurus, or service providers that offer or sell a list of "best-selling products on Amazon." If you see someone selling or giving "product ideas in fashion", you should flee

There is a huge market for courses, gurus and consulting services for Amazon sellers. And it's not hard to understand why. Amazon can be, to say the least, confusing, and people want to know how they can succeed. The problem is that there can be oversaturated markets if everyone seeks the same advice, especially on products. This means that it can be extremely difficult to generate visibility and revenue. A market can be great, but if a few hundred sellers all purchase the same product, the supply may exceed demand, resulting in fierce competition and too much inventory to be sold.

2. Following Trend Markets

Do the same for the fashionable markets as you did with the gurus and the best product lists - Run! Tracking trends can be extremely risky especially as a new seller. They are only really profitable for those who are really early for the party.

By the end of 2017, the wriggling spinner has brought a lot of money to the first sellers. But as more and more people traveled by train, demand collapsed and a lot of money was lost. Imagine it: If a product is in trend on social media or on TV, you're probably too late for the party. Even if a market seems unbelievable, with tons of sellers moving thousands of units with little overhead, you probably will not have enough time to profit from it. In the short term, it will take you two months to market your product. And at this point, public hype will gradually subside.

When you enter a market that is quickly saturated, many sellers get into price struggles with their competitors, which limits their profit margins. This can cause you to sell below the cost and lose money.

People using a trend market are very lucky with timing or they have a low cost (ie a manufacturer) or a ton of capital to invest in a product to secure the ranking. Everyone is likely to suffer a financial blow.

3. No in-depth research on restrictions/obstacles for your desired market

There are many classifications on Amazon that require an approval process to begin the sale. For these categories, you may be required to submit formal papers and statements. You may also have to pay an upfront fee to sell in the category. This can be catastrophic for new sellers who want to quickly move into a category and start selling. Make sure that you have taken the hours needed to understand the categories that require this prior work by consulting the Amazon approval process. In addition, there are special products with different restrictive barriers.

4. Procurement of low-quality products

If you want to sell a private label product, make sure it is of high quality. Buying a bad quality product can break your Amazon business from the start. Criticism is extremely difficult to generate on Amazon, and some negative reviews can clear a list at lightning speed. Take time to order samples and analyze durability, functionality and overall quality to resolve concerns that may lead to buyer complaints. Also, take the time to read the negative reviews of your competitors and see if there are any problems that you can improve. You may even want to buy some of your competitor's products to compare them to your samples and to check their quality.

5. Procurement of an expensive product (for this market)

Another thing to consider is the hidden cost of starting a private label business. As long as the sales process has not started, it may be difficult to understand all the costs associated with an FBA business. Between shipping, procurement, Amazon fees, PPC, promotions, ad creation and more, many costs have to be considered before you get started. Viral Launch has a tool that allows you an initial cost estimate can be made. Amazon also has extensive resources on referral fees and shipping costs that you need to check before launching.

If it is extremely important to have a high-quality product, if you can not beat or beat the majority of your competitors in price, then it probably is not beneficial to enter the market. We recommend that you make sure you break even by selling at a lower price than anyone else on the first page. This is not mandatory, but gives you some flexibility to adjust prices to market fluctuations.

Keep in mind that it's extremely difficult to sell a more expensive, quality-based item on Amazon when quality matters. They have limited space for copying and pictures. Buyers usually look for low prices.

6. Sell a product that you have a passion for

This could surprise people. Some may be interested in selling a product that you know or like passionately, but it can often do more harm than good. Buying a product that you have a passion for can hurt your judgment, lead to price mistakes, and make salvation difficult if a product simply does not sell. While it is not a mistake to sell something that you are passionate about, it can make you react emotionally and not logically. So remember to focus on the end result.

7. Do not inspect a product

This is another clue for private label sellers that goes along with finding a low-quality product defect. It is important that the product from the production line and your customers is in good condition and of good quality. Many sellers hire an inspection agency to oversee the manufacturing process, inspect the inventory and monitor defects and deficiencies. This step will save you so much time and money by detecting errors before the inventory is sent to the US or Amazon.

8. Procurement of a patented product

When looking for branded products from a manufacturer, it is important to consider patents. In some cases sellers have a patented product manufactured. Probably the manufacturers you buy from do not know that the product is patented and will try to sell it to anyone who buys it. That does not mean that it's legal. Imagine you are investing a lot of capital in the inventory of products to obtain the hiring and withdrawal or prosecution of the patentee.

9. Do not bother enough to make your list (including photos)

If you sell private labels, you own the product list. This means you have to configure it. You have made great efforts to find and find your next great product. It would make sense to make the same effort to create your entry, right? Unfortunately, many Amazon sellers do not join this thought. Between your photos, titles, chips, and product descriptions, you do not have much space to grab a customer's attention and explain what your product is. That's why it's so important to use the small space you have.

An effective list copy serves two purposes. It offers a compelling sales copy and helps you to index valuable keywords. Before creating a list, make sure that you thoroughly research the keywords. Find the most relevant keywords for your product and make sure they're on your list, especially the title and bullets. Make sure you write an attractive and accurate copy for your product. If you do not know how to make your own copy, read the Optimizing Viral Launch Lists service.

In terms of photography, many sellers think that taking a photo on a smartphone and a few clicks in Photoshop is the trick, but they are wrong. Professional photography can play a big role in the success or failure of a product on Amazon. Since Amazon is a very crowded market and you have limited space to sell customers for your product, high-quality photos can significantly increase sales.

10. Violation of the Terms of Use (with criticism or attacks on the competition)

Many companies launch different "black hat" strategies (in terms of use). Most of them focus on generating comments. Although these strategies may seem tempting, Amazon applies a strict strategy for generating revisions. If you are caught (or incited) by critics, you are jeopardizing your sales rights. The tactic of handling notifications is common on Amazon, and many sellers initially have big problems. However, Amazon has strongly opposed consultant fraud, and the impact can be extremely damaging to your business.

11. Do not monitor your list or data

For private label sellers, your list of products resembles a living, functioning person. There are many ups and downs and changes from one day to the next. Far too many private label sellers publish their list and believe that they are ready. It's important to continue monitoring your collection to collect data and see how it works. You also need to track the evolution of the list of competitors and the entire category. Also, make sure you monitor your rankings for key keywords and campaign data and use that information to develop a long-term strategy. Getting your list is only half the battle. Comment-based adjustments and optimizations are the other half.

12. Put your product in the wrong category

As a private label supplier, creating a product list involves determining the category in which your product is listed. During this step, it is important that you place your product in the appropriate category. Some sellers try to classify their products in a less competitive market to get the bestseller badge. However, many searches filter for a specific subcategory. As a result, incorrect categorization of your product can prevent you from receiving important search results.

Sellers can view their product in Seller Central to identify potential categories. Just make sure your product matches the one you've selected.

Pre-Purchase Errors:

1. Not Recognizing The Amazon Marketplace Idea

Selling on Amazon is not like other channels where an organization can sell its products. Amazon created the third-party marketplace to supplement its Amazon Retail business, where it sources products directly from brands.

The Marketplace Allows Amazon to Organize Data and lots Of Data

Through the millions of individuals doing billions of transactions every year, Amazon Retail can get difficult and broad data on customer desires, using that data itself to create its sourcing strategy for the coming years.

Because it does not share this data with third-party sellers, Amazon Retail has the massive benefits of being able to "cherry-pick" brands and specific SKUs that it can see are already becoming favorites among Amazon customers. By acting on this data, Amazon can continually take control of the sales of top-selling items, previously sold only by Amazon third-party sellers.

Since the marketplace designs products so all the sellers of the same item show up on the same merchandise listing page, it is easier for customers to examine offers of the same item, choosing what they believe is best for them (concerning availability, pricing, delivery time, etc).

The Consequence Of the amazon Buy Box Algorithm

Layered onto this single-SKU structure is Amazon's "Buy Box Algorithm", the algorithm that determines which seller will have its items added to the consumer's cart when the customer clicks the purchase button.

Indeed, this "Buy Box Algorithm" is so consequential that it is very silly for any organization to think of buying an Amazon seller account without a fundamental understanding of how the algorithm operates. Without this knowledge, a seller may find himself with lots of merchandise that he will never sell because other dealers dominate the Buy Box on those particular items.

You should not think of acquiring an Amazon Seller business without understanding the Buy Box.

FBA Sellers Get a Buy Box Algorithm Boost

Amazon wants to develop a fluent, regular, top-notch experience for shoppers, every single time the customer shops on Amazon. While the Buy Box algorithm assesses each seller's preceding accomplishments with regards to such criteria as punctuality with delivery, inclination to reverse orders, and feedback reviews, the algorithm also remunerates the seller that chooses to make use of Amazon Fulfillment by Amazon (FBA) program.

The FBA program empowers sellers to send goods in bulk to Amazon's fulfillment stations, thereby causing their products to be qualified for PRIME Shipping and Super-Saver Shipping – two fast shipping arrangements that enable Amazon to assure customers of consistently accelerated delivery of their purchases.

But with incorporation into the FBA program also comes the condition that merchants accept Amazon's very kind refund policy – a policy at times so tolerant that new retailers will be shocked by how easy some consumers get away with obvious customer fraud. However, this costlier cost of returns is typically offset with superior consumer conversion resulting from merchandises being in the FBA program.

New sellers on Amazon should note that the marketplace is a quickly-evolving market where rivals are not always rational, where the number of competitors on specific listings can improve significantly overnight (leading to dropping sales and margins), and where Amazon Retail has the constant advantage over all the other sellers.

Furthermore, what an organization or seller offers today in its stock is likely going to change over time as the rivalry on particular items changes. We have observed sellers be particularly prosperous by getting private sourcing deals on influential products, or developing very tuned functional skills that permit them to get in and out of products without too many problems around old inventory, high-interest rates and fade margins.

2. They Do not Secure Key Brands In Writing

When a merchant account is made open for sale, it's crucial for the buyer to understand which goods carried are curated through exclusive relationships with the brand.

Those products that do come with particular curating deals in place (versus a model of anyone can curate the items from the brand or distributor), it is important that the buyer receives written evidence that it will be able to continue sourcing these brands. Otherwise, it's entirely conceivable that new owners will find themselves cut off by the brands soon after they finish the account selling process.

3. Not Understand Which Items Are Essential Drivers Of Profit and Loss

Equally significant to securing sourcing relationships is recognizing the SKU-level profitability of the trade being bought. We have seen companies purchase seller accounts without a definite understanding of which parts of the catalog are making money, and which are not.

Many sellers of Amazon accounts organize the account before the purchase by improving top-line revenues quickly (at the expense of the bottom line). So it is important that the account buyer understands at a very minute level which SKUs produce profits and losses today.

4. Inadequately Accounting For Contracts From Uncollected/Remitted State Tax & Customs Duties

Not all Amazon sellers are efficient and put together concerning state taxes. With the nexus tax meanings of Amazon's FBA program not well known, a lot of sellers are not properly handling and paying sales tax in all states where they have produced tax nexus. It is best to get a tax lawyer to evaluate a target seller business prior to the sale so as to avoid an expensive bill for back taxes in the future.

Likewise, if the current Amazon seller imports merchandise from overseas, it is very prudent to examine the import duties paid in the preceding two years on the account. We have seen circumstances where merchandises were misclassified in the past when imported, ending in tax fines when US Customs identified the errors

Post-Purchase Errors:

1. Significant Revisions To Functional Operations & Fulfillment That Lead To Reduction Of Performance Metrics

I mentioned earlier that handling an Amazon seller account will demand an understanding of and adherence to all merchant performance metrics that Amazon tracks. The key point for recent buyers of Amazon accounts is to understand precisely what actions are needed to ensure these performance metrics persist strongly.

Realistically, the best plan of action is to demand that the seller of the Amazon account render at least one week of hands-on training, teaching the business specifics that affect these Amazon performance metrics. As with a brand-new seller accounts, Amazon does not afford a new seller with any space to prepare and get used to the high metrics, so it is fitting to include some hand-holding during the handoff to guarantee a smooth transition.

It is also advised that new users prepare for a lot more work managing the day-to-day processes that they have encountered with other sorts of businesses.

2. Not Understand Where Growth Possibilities Are

Finally, while an Amazon seller account may present a new buyer with decent projected cash flows, it is crucial for this buyer to understand precisely where the possibilities are to develop and build the business.

Due to intensified opposition each year, an Amazon seller can expect to have to work harder to keep the same boundaries. So without a distinct plan of how and where to find growth, too many new users of Amazon sellers accounts will become quickly discouraged by how much work they are planting into the business, only to see predicted margins fading away month by month.

3. Not Adjusting to a Changing Tax Nexus Position

A seller account had a nexus tax category before, but with the shift to another owner, the tax nexus position may well change, leaving the new owner opened to uncollected sales taxes. It is important that any updates to sales tax nexus be made promptly upon transfer of control to avoid accumulated tax liabilities while the new owners understand out what's going on.

SELLING ON AMAZON: CHALLENGES AND OPPORTUNITIES

When you think about selling at Amazon, it's important to be realistic. Do not expect your products to fly off virtual shelves just because you are putting them up at Amazon. The Amazon catalog contains more than 400 million products. The 400 millionth and first product you add to the catalog will not be noticed immediately. If you want to create sales on Amazon, you need to determine how to increase traffic to your ads.

Will you promote paid advertising on Amazon or Facebook? Send an e-mail to customers to let them know about your membership on Amazon?

The Cannibalization Myth of Sale

When considering selling to Amazon, many brands are concerned about being able to exclude traffic from their own website.

The truth is this - there are not many brands in the world who have as large a customer base as Amazon. If you understand just how massive Amazon's customer base is, you will realize that the revenues you generate can far exceed anything you'll ever achieve on your own website.

You may spend a lot of money today to increase traffic to your site but it is a guaranteed fact that Amazon generates the same traffic on its website more efficiently. You'll still need to spend more than Amazon to get similar results.

The hard reality is that Amazon does not care about your product as the market is likely to have 10 other similar products and sell one of these 10 products. You need to decide if you want to get a small piece of a large cake or 100% of a cupcake on your own website. For many brands, the solution is to pursue both. Making this decision can mean understanding that there are already enough competitors on Amazon and they do not want to be left behind.

Dive into the strategy (and why it does not work)

If you develop your business on your own website and use it as your primary channel, you probably will not be ready to sell on Amazon. You can try a few things with one or two products without completely subscribing to the idea. Part of the challenge, however, is that it's difficult to get to the top of Amazon with a single product and expect to take full advantage of the list and or create enough traffic to start a successful selling. There is a significant time when you have to say:

"If we sell on Amazon, we will do it right. We've all put away our content and blocked it, so at least we know that they are of high quality when someone else tries to sell them. "

It's a good idea to place a variety of products on Amazon rather than just one or two. If you put up one or two products on Amazon, you probably will not invest the time and money required to succeed. Essentially, it is a website with 400 million other products competing for attention. To be successful, you need to focus on generating laser traffic and laser attention for these products on Amazon.

Remember, there are already more than two million Amazon sellers. Even if you only take 1% of the bestsellers, there are 20,000 sellers who know how to play the game and refine Amazon's sales strategies for years.

Most of these sellers know how to travel to Asia and supply as needed. It's important to determine how to make your ads good enough to compete with the best 1% of bestsellers with the means and experience to recreate your product. These sellers bypass patents, designs, and brands so Amazon customers can see and buy their product version before they see it, since they spend only $ 100 apiece per month to attract 20 people.

The worst solution: fake ignorance

The worst way to sell on Amazon is to pretend that the problem of unauthorized sellers disappears soon. The problem will only worsen and pollute all other channels where your brand is trying to sell.

Brands often think of themselves, "I have my own website and two or three retailers, so let's get started." This is a losing strategy - a sure way to fail at it.

Amazon is here to stay. Therefore, it is important to understand that customers are actively watching your products to learn how to create less expensive versions. They also know how to sell it better than you. Do not wait to be disturbed by this.

Unless you have an extraordinary loyalty to a distinctively unique product and the only place where people can buy it is someone on your site or in a channel that you control closely (like in a franchise) Amazon can help you make a cheaper and more functional version of the same item and get a lot of revenue before Amazon becomes a major channel for your business.

The right approach for selling on Amazon

A brand needs to control its prices, and to control your prices you need to control your distribution. To control your distribution, you must have the appropriate brand as we have already discussed.

However, it turns out that Amazon Retail, the company's first supplier, reviews your product if your brand is sufficiently known and successful. You think: "We could buy pallets from this TLC and sell them on our site, in fact we know that many Amazon customers are looking for them and can not find them, so we'll look for them." Thus, Amazon Retail connects directly with a brand and buys many products.

B2B companies are happy because they understand how they make B2B sales, but they do not understand that Amazon is a very big channel that can negatively affect their ability to achieve consistent pricing across channels, as Amazon does can also decide to lower prices.

Amazon does not have to make money selling your brand. They only have to satisfy customers who come back to buy the product.

Now, let us examine the model that works.

The hybrid model (ie the successful model)

Amazon sells best with a hybrid model, where part of your catalog is sold as the first part and another part. Here are several aspects to consider.

First, for your best-selling products, Amazon is likely to find a way to get that product anyway. If they can not buy it directly from you, they go to one of your dealers and buy the bought products. Or find a foreign distributor you can not really control, and ask him to re-import the product.

Now Amazon Retail offers a first-class product that you have not even sold and you are not even included in the conversation with them. If you have proprietary and third-party products, this hybrid model gives you access to a variety of marketing programs.

Accessing Amazon tools and data

Amazon offers a variety of programs for third-party vendors and sellers. If you have products in both cases, you really have access to all the marketing tools. In this way, you can generate traffic in different ways and move products from one model to another.

It is important to know that as a reseller, you only restore the number of units sold by Amazon. If you're a third-party, you can at least know how many units of each product were sold per order, so you can capture more customer data. The customer relationship is not yours, but you can get more information that will allow you to experiment with many different types of bundles, which is very difficult on the provider side. Essentially, the hybrid model gives your company more flexibility. This is therefore the approach that is recommended to get the most out of Amazon.

Last thoughts

There is no miracle solution for selling on Amazon, but Amazon is here to stay. If you work long term, you have to consider Amazon as a channel of communication, a channel of distribution and advertising channel. It's really all three. And if you think long term, you'll need to look at what's happening to your brand on Amazon.

Think of Amazon as blocking your content and promoting your products to a large number of customers. And if you have not done so by now, it's time to start a serious discussion on how to control the distribution.

Do you sell a product to someone who comes with an order? Do you recognize the downstream effects that cause this Amazon Channel issue? In many ways, Amazon is a wake-up call to ask you:

"Am I really a serious brand that wants to be in about five years?" In that case, you must immediately take control of your brand, distribution and prices. The faster you turn to the Amazon channel, the faster you become a disciplined brand ready to win on every channel you sell.

CONCLUSIONS

Running an Amazon seller business must be handled as a daily activity. While prospective buyers may see the acquisition of an existing Amazon account as a smart way to get into e-commerce, or as a way to make some satisfactory cash flow each month, much Amazon-specific due attention is required beforehand. A method for producing quick subject matter expertise on the Amazon marketplace is vital to ensuring that there are not harmful mistakes early into the new ownership.

In fact, this high bar for performance metrics is a primary factor for Amazon's policy restricting the sale of Amazon seller accounts. Of course, any seller is certainly free to offer for sale its know-how, existing inventory and sourcing relationships to another organization (though Amazon requires that a new seller account be set up by the new buyer.

11821701R00139